CONTENTS

For everyone who has ever believed that they could change the world; my husband, whose loving heart and support sustains me; and my furry, four-footed children, who show me what absolute faith and joy are every day on their walks.

—Paige H. Teegarden

For Larry, who makes everything possible; Edgar, who was my greatest cheerleader; my parents, who introduced me to giving generously; and Maxine, who inspired my understanding of how organizations work.

—Denice R. Hinden

For Jennifer . . . and for everyone who works or volunteers in the nonprofit sector. You are the heart and soul of your communities and our society.

—Paul Sturm

"This is an important book for consultants and managers who work with nonprofit organizations. *The Nonprofit Organizational Culture Guide* lays out basic theory about how nonprofits come to be and how they operate, and it demonstrates how important the concept of culture is to understanding this important sector of our society."

—Edgar H. Schein, professor of management, emeritus, MIT Sloan School of Management

"This book is a must-read for nonprofit executives! The authors spell out the themes, beliefs, and assumptions that are unique to nonprofits, regardless of their size or mission, ultimately revealing how 'culture' manifests itself in organizations."

—Darryl A. Jones, Sr., CEO, Maryland Association of Nonprofit Organizations

"This is a groundbreaking work. Readers will find a practical methodology for assessing organizational culture and a helpful framework for classifying the 'stories' behind their nonprofits."

—Frank Omowale Satterwhite, founder and senior adviser, National Community Development Institute

"This is the book that the nonprofit community has needed for a long time. The authors provide a compelling assessment tool that all organizations can use. This book is essential to understanding how nonprofits work and why they do or do not achieve the outcomes and missions they set for themselves."

—Flo Green, vice president, IdeaEncore Network

"Anyone who works in a group and relies on others to get things done will benefit from this book. Readers will discover how the environment of an organization influences how decisions are made and, ultimately, how things get done."

—Natalie Abatemarco, director of North America community programs, Citigroup, Inc.

"*The Nonprofit Organizational Culture Guide* offers a new view of culture within the nonprofit sector. It combines research and practical tools for practitioners who want to understand the abstract topic of organizational culture."

—Sarah Mullins, consultant, Dare Mighty Things

"Every organization has culture, recognized or not. And that culture plays a powerful role in shaping the way people act within that context. The insights, frameworks, and tools in this book will help people become more astute within their organizational cultures."

—Brian Fraser, lead provocateur, Jazzthink

The Nonprofit Organizational Culture Guide

REVEALING THE HIDDEN TRUTHS
THAT IMPACT PERFORMANCE

Paige Hull Teegarden
Denice Rothman Hinden
Paul Sturm

Foreword by
Peter Brinckerhoff

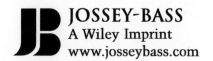

JOSSEY-BASS
A Wiley Imprint
www.josseybass.com

Published by Jossey-Bass
A Wiley Imprint
989 Market Street, San Francisco, CA 94103-1741—www.josseybass.com

Jossey-Bass books and products are available through most bookstores. To contact Jossey-Bass directly call our Customer Care Department within the U.S. at 800-956-7739, outside the U.S. at 317-572-3986, or fax 317-572-4002.

Jossey-Bass also publishes its books in a variety of electronic formats. Some content that appears in print may not be available in electronic books.

Library of Congress Cataloging-in-Publication Data

Teegarden, Paige Hull.
    The nonprofit organizational culture guide: revealing the hidden truths that impact performance/ Paige Hull Teegarden, Denice Rothman Hinden, Paul Sturm; foreword by Peter Brinckerhoff.
      p.   cm.
    Includes bibliographical references and index.
    ISBN 978-0-470-89154-4 (pbk.)
      1. Nonprofit organizations—Management. 2. Corporate culture. 3. Performance. I. Hinden, Denice Rothman. II. Sturm, Paul. III. Title.
    HD62.6.T443   2011
    658.3'14—dc22

                                                                                          2010037987

Printed in the United States of America
FIRST EDITION
PB Printing   10 9 8 7 6 5 4 3 2 1

LIST OF TABLES, FIGURES, AND EXHIBITS

FOUR

FIVE

FOREWORD

Nonprofits are different. Or unique. Or special. Or wonderful. Take your pick. But those of us who labor in and around mission-based organizations know that once you have had a mission, it's impossible to go back to having just a job. So we stay, and often become lifers helping achieve our nonprofit's mission.

We hardly ever labor alone. Within our nonprofit, we work with other staff, boards of directors, and nongoverning volunteers. And our organization has a history, whether it started in 1910 or 2005. Over time it has developed traditions, stories, successes, and setbacks, the life scars of any nonprofit. All these things contribute to our nonprofit's unique culture.

A wise nonprofit executive director once told me that there were just two reasons our staff and volunteers show up each day: "Our mission, and the way we treat each other." That truth has stuck with me over the years, and formed much of my thinking about nonprofit management and internal staff and volunteer development. We need each other to pursue our mission. We need to understand each other and our environment to pursue our mission more effectively and efficiently. That means we need to both recognize and understand our culture.

It always intrigues me that although nonprofits have been leaders in becoming culturally competent with the many cultures of their geographic communities, often they are not as adept at figuring out how to be culturally competent inside their organization. Whereas in the past this situation may have been for lack of good tools, it no longer needs to be. The book you are about to read is full of what every nonprofit leader needs to understand about his or her organizational culture and to create an even better one.

The job of a nonprofit steward is to use all the resources of the organization to get more and better mission out the door each day. The culture of a nonprofit is just such a resource, one that until now was not fully decipherable. What you read in the following pages will help you decode and improve your organization's culture and, as a result, help you develop a more mission-capable organization. Good luck.

Peter Brinckerhoff
Author, *Mission-Based Management*
President, Corporate Alternatives
peter@missionbased.com

Are any of these situations familiar to you?

A nonprofit organization hires a new executive director with a record of success in a similar role in other nonprofits. After less than a year, the board decides to make a change, concluding that the executive director was "not the right fit for our organization."

A consultant is retained to facilitate development of a new strategic plan for a nonprofit organization. Although the completed plan contains goals, objectives, and work plans that look good on paper, the plan winds up sitting on the shelf, leaving board members scratching their heads and swearing never to do strategic planning again.

Two executives from local corporations are recruited by a nonprofit organization as new members of its board of directors. After three meetings, they quit the board in frustration, believing that their input is neither valued nor wanted by the organization.

The local community foundation provides a grant to two nonprofit organizations with the stipulation that they collaborate to carry out the funded project. After six months, the project is bogged down. The executive directors of both organizations accuse each other of acting in bad faith and ask the foundation to withdraw the other organization's portion of the grant.

If, like us, you've witnessed these or similar events, you'll understand why we came to believe that something was missing in the nonprofit management literature and, therefore, that more was needed to enhance the toolkits of nonprofit leaders and capacity builders. Paul Light, the Paulette Goddard Professor of Public Service at New York University, reinforced this for us when he wrote, "There appear to be plenty of well-managed nonprofits that do not make a programmatic difference, and plenty of organizations that make a programmatic difference in spite of poor management" (2002, p. 39).

When we first read Light's assertion, it raised a number of questions:

If the quality of management is not the determining factor in the effectiveness of nonprofit organizations, what is it that ultimately separates effective nonprofits from ineffective ones?

Is there something less tangible and measurable, perhaps beneath the surface, that explains why some nonprofits thrive while others struggle merely to survive?

Could we come up with a way to see what is unseen but unmistakably in the air within nonprofit organizations? That is, could we unearth the *hidden truths* that seem to govern how an organization functions?

Could we develop a method to help nonprofit leaders and capacity builders understand the elusive traits embedded in the character and reflected in the behavior of a nonprofit organization?

If so, could we find sufficient evidence in the literature of anthropology, sociology, psychology, and business to justify calling our work the discovery of nonprofit organizational culture?

After a collective journey on a road that turned many corners and lasted over five years, the answer is "Yes, we can!" And although we have traveled and explored together over these last five years, our individual journeys began in different places.

For Denice, leading a capacity-building initiative with fourteen community development corporations in Indianapolis marked a turning point in her thinking about how to help improve nonprofit organizations. The organizations were physically close to each other but unique in every way. Denice and a team of consultants, with varied experience in designing and carrying out customized organizational capacity-building activities, assessed each organization's development needs. The results were instructive. A few organizations wrote their first strategic plan or a fundraising plan; others renewed or updated personnel policies and operating procedures. However, a majority of organizations did not receive anything of long-term value for their leadership, management, board development, or fundraising. Many finished the project with an unsettled feeling or an unsatisfactory experience. In retrospect, Denice realized that this work did not include discussions about organizational culture or about how understanding it could make a difference in the life of these organizations.

For Paul, the experiences of working with two pairs of nonprofit organizations—one pair locally based, the other pair national—with similar missions but very different results triggered much reflection, followed by conversations with colleagues to better understand why the results of organizations that looked so similar on the surface were so different.

Of the local pair, one organization had a sizable budget and staff; it had been in existence nearly thirty years. The second was considerably smaller and much newer. The conventional indicators of money and size would lead one to conclude that the first organization would have much greater impact and more impressive results than the second.

The conventional indicators would be wrong. It was the smaller of the two organizations that made the bigger difference. Its programs reached greater numbers of individuals, and its documented outcomes far surpassed those of the larger organization. What accounted for the counterintuitive results of the two organizations? Reflecting on this phenomenon, Paul saw that the answer was in the very different cultures of the two organizations.

At the time, many people in the community experienced the larger organization as having a "culture of conflict." Leadership had a strong sense of turf and territory, believing that it was the only organization with the right to deliver programs and services in its mission area. The organization's leadership viewed groups with related missions or interest in the recipients of its programs as adversaries to be undermined and attacked, and staff were expected to act accordingly. The environment within the organization suggested a place engaged in constant battle. And this sense of battle used up a considerable amount of the organization's resources—financial as well as emotional—thereby reducing resources available to carry out the organization's mission and deliver its programs.

In contrast, the smaller organization built a "culture of collaboration." Leadership continually reached out and asked others to join the organization in planning and implementing programs for the benefit of the community. Virtually all programs were planned and implemented in partnership with one or more other entities. This enabled the organization to leverage resources and bring a broad array of programs to its constituency. Staff time and energy were spent in the affirming work of service rather than the draining work of conflict.

At about the same time, Paul observed organizational culture and its impact up close through the lens of two national associations. Like the two local organizations, one had a much greater supply of financial resources and paid staff than the other. The larger one was the result of a merger between the smaller one and another organization with a similar mission. And similar to the other situation, the contrast in the two organizational cultures and results was as stark as night and day.

The original association had a clear "culture of community." The organization had no full-time staff and or physical office of its own, so activities were driven and shaped by the needs and resourcefulness of its members. Annual conferences were designed to create community in a variety of ways that engaged the hearts, souls, and senses of participants, who felt celebrated, affirmed, and energized. An extraordinary amount of activity was carried out throughout the year by association members to support, serve, and strengthen their work. Board members were elected by the association's membership in an open and participatory process. It was a culture that truly affirmed and empowered its members.

In contrast, the association created by the merger approached its work very differently. A sizable amount of money was raised to support staff at a central office. Rather than being elected by membership in an open meeting, board members were appointed by a small group in a closed process. An especially telling symbol of how the culture changed from the original to the merged organization was visible at the closing session of the new organization's first conference, when board members were seated at a raised table looking down on the membership. This was in stark contrast to the original association, where board members were seated at the tables with other members during the conference closing sessions. The culture had shifted, and the message was unmistakable!

For Paige, she experienced a "crisis of faith" after several years as a consultant to nonprofit organizations. Wondering if she was helping her clients in a deep and meaningful way, Paige asked herself how many would ultimately make significant changes, at a deep level, in what they did or how they did it, particularly when there was a pressing reason to do so.

Far too often, she observed organizations that were standing at the precipice of change turn back—or take tentative steps, only to turn back quickly. She wondered if these were manifestations of the natural tendency of humans to avoid change. However, over time, Paige noticed something else. She noticed what staff and board members did not say. She noticed that often, at some point during decision making, there were walls in people's minds. There were possibilities that from the outside looked real, but from the inside were untenable. And, often, people could not explain why the possibilities seemed impossible.

Moreover, Paige noticed that board and staff spoke about their organization's values as aspirational. They talked about how they wanted the organization to be seen or the values they thought should be important. They often talked about teamwork or collaboration or shared leadership because these are *supposed to be* values in nonprofits. But in many cases, these same nonprofits defended turf and ultimately acted in ways that were not at all collaborative. They'd talk about the critical role staff plays, but not increase compensation or provide an option for flexible work hours. Why, she wondered, did these often successful organizations act in this manner?

Eventually, Paige and her colleagues started asking about stories that connected people to the organization. They asked staff to share stories about interactions with one another that illustrated a particularly successful project and why it was successful. These stories and others brought to light the values that were actually operating. These were the first glimpses at organizational culture. Understanding these stories and values may not have made these clients more able to make changes, but they did deeply describe the heart of their organization and began to show why certain options and possibilities were "untenable."

The need and level of interest for this book further crystallized in July 2003, when Denice and Paul facilitated a breakfast roundtable at the Alliance for Nonprofit Management's annual conference in Houston. It was the largest roundtable of that conference, with the number of participants limited only by how many could squeeze around two tables moved together. The discussion was lively and helped us generate the following questions:

- How does organizational culture affect the potential of an organization to achieve its vision?
- Where is the leadership and management opportunity if the organizational culture and vision are not in sync?
- How do we describe organizational culture in such a way that it is useful and connected to the organization's strengths?

- Is organizational culture changeable?

- How do we make organizational culture something that leaders and managers understand and accept in a nonblaming, nonpersonal way rather than as something to be "fixed" or "removed" from an organization?

- How do we consider organizational culture as a factor in measuring organization performance?

Over the course of researching and writing this book, the three of us have each contributed something unique that makes the whole greater than the sum of its parts. From day one, Paige brought her unrelentingly probing and analytical mind. Asking "tell me more" and challenging her coauthors to go deeper with their thoughts and ideas, Paige always wants to know the story behind the facts and the history behind the story. Paige also connected ideas—hers and ours—into a coherent whole. Whether it was a new way of analyzing existing literature and theories, understanding why stories were critical, or offering a new perspective on processes, Paige brought creativity, rigor, and structure to our work.

Paul brought the fierce pragmatism of someone whose life has focused on transforming the visions of what could be into the workable realities of what is. Throughout our work together, Paul was always asking how what we've learned can be best understood and used by nonprofit leaders, capacity builders, and other readers. Paul also supplied a rich array of experiences to reflect on and against which to test our evolving ideas about nonprofit organizational culture.

Denice's natural intellectual rigor and honesty kept us from taking too many leaps off the cliffs on which we occasionally found ourselves. Repeatedly asking for the evidence to support our statements and conclusions, Denice allowed us to assure you that the book is grounded in the reality of what we've experienced, observed, learned from the research, or carefully thought through. Denice's thoughtful comments and questions helped hold us close to the core purpose of the work. Denice, through Managance Consulting & Coaching, also provided a home base and institutional support for our work.

Perhaps most important, we all bring a passion for the nonprofit sector and a belief that the work which ultimately makes the greatest difference in the quality of human and community life is carried out each day by the staff and volunteers of nonprofit organizations. The fire that led each of us into the nonprofit sector burns as deeply as ever, as does our desire to contribute what we've learned in the course of our research and writing the book.

We realize that understanding organizational culture in nonprofits requires time to be reflective and willingness to look at ideas that grow first from intuition rather than hard science. It is time well worth taking because to truly understand nonprofit organizations, one must understand their unique organizational cultures. As our research for the book reinforced over and over, an organization's culture lives in its walk, not its talk; in its accepted practices, not its written policies. It does not reside in official pronouncements or platitudes. It lives in the day-to-day conversations and interactions among staff members, in the subtle but unmistakable messages as to what is really valued by the organization, in the ways in which new ideas and initiatives are resisted or supported by professional and volunteer leadership.

It is this lens and perspective that we believe our book brings to nonprofit leaders, managers, capacity builders, and educators. We hope the book will not only help us all better understand nonprofit organizations but, ultimately, enable nonprofits to carry out their vital work at the highest levels of impact and effectiveness. The process of understanding organizational culture has much to teach us about how to shape sustainable organizations of which people want to be part and to build the capacity of organizations to effectively fulfill their missions and make their intended difference in the quality of human and community life.

November 2010

Paige Hull Teegarden
Denice Rothman Hinden
Paul Sturm

Introduction
How to Get at Hidden Truths

This book explores the nature of organizational culture in primarily human service and community service nonprofit organizations. It takes the position that organizational culture is real, pervasive, and complex—and that it matters. It also takes the position that organizational culture is often misunderstood and that by embracing a new mind-set about what it is and how to use it, leaders can use organizational culture as a powerful management tool. We believe that in spite of its elusive nature, organizational culture offers a new, important perspective for leaders of nonprofit organizations.

Most important, this book introduces our process for uncovering the hidden truths that govern organizational behavior. Our Revealing Organizational Culture process (ROC) is a step-by-step guide for discovering elements of organizational culture and developing strategies for applying those discoveries to management challenges.

This is a handbook—part reference tool, part practical guide—for nonprofit managers and leaders, board members, consultants, and funders, as well as for nonprofit management educators and others who seek to help nonprofits improve their organizations, service delivery, and performance in accomplishing their missions.

Why should you care about organizational culture? What is organizational culture? Can understanding organizational culture help you better lead and manage your organization or better help you offer sound advice and counsel to nonprofits? We hope this book will help you begin to answer these questions by

• Exploring the meaning of organizational culture

- Reviewing alternative ways of surfacing the organizational culture in a non-profit organization
- Understanding how paying attention to organizational culture can be valuable in the context of managing nonprofit organizations

We have heard two additional uses of the term *culture* in the nonprofit sector that deserve a brief mention here. The first is the term *cultural competency*, which refers to the ability to interact effectively and appropriately with people of different cultures. This is a traditional use of the term *culture* and refers to the broad cultures—regional, ethnic, religious—that have a strong impact on an individual's worldview and behavior. It is simply a different term and does not directly bear on this exploration.

The second usage of the term culture is descriptive of organizational practices, such as "we have a culture of entrepreneurship" or "we'd like to create a culture of inquiry." In this use, people are trying to describe a characteristic of the way the organization operates or wishes to operate. This usage often has an aspirational sense attached to a practice—the particular practice (entrepreneurship or inquiry) is something board, staff, consultants, or funders would like to see increased and supported in the organization. This use is clearly related to the meaning we're exploring in this book. However, like the many references to organizational culture in the nonprofit literature, its use is vague and may sometimes express a wish that is contrary to the organization's deepest cultural impulses.

HOW THIS BOOK IS ORGANIZED

We wrote this book with many audiences in mind: nonprofit organization leaders, capacity builders, nonprofit management educators and scholars, funders, and others who are interested in the nonprofit sector's effectiveness.

In Chapter One, we explore the academic and management literature about organizational culture. With information about the history and development of the concept of organizational culture, we aim to deepen your understanding of what organizational culture is and why it so widely referenced.

We make three critical arguments about nonprofit organizational culture. First, the definition of organizational culture in nonprofits is the same as the definition for public or for-profit organizations—organizational culture is organizational culture no matter the context. Second, we do not believe there is a specific organizational culture that is critical to nonprofit effectiveness. In other words, there is no "perfect culture" that all nonprofits should try to achieve. Each organization's culture must be understood on its own terms, including its strengths and challenges. Further, what is effective for each organization will be unique to its culture.

_____

There is no "perfect culture" that all nonprofits should try to achieve. Each organization's culture must be understood on its own terms, including its strengths and challenges. What is effective for each organization will be unique to its culture.

_____

Third, we argue that there are commonalities across many nonprofit organizations' cultures that arise from the theoretical, legal, and situational boundaries that distinguish nonprofit organizations from other types of organizational structures. Although these commonalities do not quite bubble up to the level of constituting a singular nonprofit sector culture, they come close. We believe that consultants, thought leaders, foundation leaders, and others who think about the nonprofit sector as a single entity will find in this chapter a unique exploration of what it means to "be nonprofit" and a sense of the broad, if hidden, truths shared by most nonprofits.

In Chapter Two, we explicitly examine organizational culture in the nonprofit sector through descriptions of six different nonprofits. Four are community-based service organizations, one is a membership organization, and one is an international development and research organization. We gathered the data from these organizations through structured telephone interviews with a key informant at each organization. Through our analysis of these interviews, we show how elements of organizational culture become more visible during particular times of stress and how a deeper understanding of these elements may begin to help an organization cope with stress or create a beneficial response to it. In other words, we show how organizational culture may be helping or hindering organization management during challenging times.

In Chapter Three, we introduce our process for Revealing Organizational Culture (ROC) and a step-by-step guide for using it. Through writing this book we discovered that understanding how to identify the true nature of organizational culture is a learned skill; it is a matter of having a cultural perspective, being able to step outside the organization and look in, and knowing where to look and what to look for. Through the ROC process, we take you through the gathering of basic information, descriptions of what happens in the organization, and group storytelling; and we help you know where to look within this information for aspects of the organization's culture. We focus on three particular kinds of stories—creation stories about the founding of the organization, survival stories about the resolution of particularly hard challenges, and hero and heroine stories about the quintessential staff and success.

Through the ROC, a participatory process, organizations discover their hidden truths and develop an organizational culture summary statement. This statement begins to articulate the deepest underlying assumptions of the organizational culture. In doing so, it provides the context for understanding how elements of the culture can help or hinder efforts to solve management challenges. It is in this understanding that organizations begin to find new ways of responding to management challenges and opportunities. Finally, we help you apply this new understanding to specific management or performance objectives.

> *Understanding how to identify the true nature of organizational culture is a learned skill; it is a matter of having a cultural perspective, being able to step outside the organization and look in, and knowing where to look and what to look for.*

In Chapter Four, we draw a distinction between the process of discovering elements of your organizational culture using the ROC and the action of applying what you learn. Through our research, we learned that the need or pressure to change organizational culture most often surfaces during times of stress or challenge in an organization. However, this is often the most difficult time to stop to reveal organizational culture. Therefore, we suggest making at least a cursory assessment of organizational culture as part of organization development activity, such as strategy development, marketing, image building, all types of capacity building, and succession planning. Then you will have the information about your organization's culture that you will need during more stressful periods, such as executive transitions, restructuring, organizational alignment, and mergers. Once an organization implements the ROC and has a baseline understanding of its organizational culture, it can repeatedly use its organizational culture summary statement to inform management strategies.

In Chapter Five, we conclude with a few recommendations for helping nonprofit leaders and capacity builders make it a habit to consider organizational culture. It is important to understand that revealing an organization's culture is an ongoing process. Opportunities to intentionally and creatively use the information to enhance organization performance will continually arise. We conclude the book with a few new questions to drive future research.

In the appendixes, we share information about people we interviewed, list the organizational culture tools and surveys that we reviewed in developing this book, and provide a little more information about mind mapping.

THE VALUE OF KNOWING YOUR ORGANIZATIONAL CULTURE

By describing and understanding organizational culture (what we call revealing organizational culture), you will be better able to fulfill your role in helping organizations perform better. You will be able to better understand the choices your organization makes and be more likely to guide successful choices. By choosing to reveal your organization's culture, you will be better able to

- Orient new staff and board members
- Find better leadership matches
- Better understand and define your theory of change
- Develop more effective strategies
- Market and communicate more effectively
- Make successful choices about restructuring or mergers

In short, by deeply appreciating what organizational culture is and taking the time to reveal it in your own organization, you will be more effective in almost every leadership and management choice you make.

Our recommendation is that once organizations invest the time to reveal their organizational culture, they would benefit further by making the information an intentional part of future management discussions and decisions. You'll notice that we aren't focused here on changing culture. Throughout this book, we are careful to acknowledge the complexity and comprehensiveness of culture. We don't think wholesale change of culture is possible without dissolving an organization. We do think adjustments that help a culture evolve in a particular direction are possible with careful, consistent attention.

Researching and writing this book has been an extraordinary experience. We hope that our work inspires you to advance what is known about organizational culture. Please join us in our ongoing quest to further understand organizational culture and how we can use what we learn to strengthen the leadership, management, and performance of nonprofit organizations.

We'd love to hear about your experiences with the ROC and your other questions about organizational culture. Visit www.revealorganizationalculture.com to join the discussion. We would like to know where the ROC is effective and where we need to work on improvements in our instructions. We also want to know how you are applying the information in your management strategies and what shifts the information helps you make in your organizational culture.

Welcome to our quest!

Nonprofit Culture

T oday, the U.S. nonprofit sector is populated by nearly two million organizations and employs approximately eleven million people. The sector as a whole—from museums, colleges, and hospitals to community centers and after-school programs—fulfills many social and community needs. Numerous scholars have indicated that nonprofit and voluntary institutions are a critical strand of America's cultural fabric.

Considering that nonprofits are such a large part of the U.S. economy and critical players in the provision of social and community services, it is not surprising that over the last several years, there has been an increasingly strong push from funders and volunteers to understand the impact nonprofits are making. Discussions of nonprofit organizational culture have become a part of this sectorwide conversation.

If you read books or popular articles about nonprofit leadership or management, you'll find plenty of references to organizational culture as something that has an impact on how institutions behave. And although ubiquitous, the term is rarely defined. Authors assume the reader will know what organizational culture is. And indeed, most of us have a sense that organizations have "cultures" that shape everything the organization does. We sense that organizational culture is powerful. We talk about it in simple terms while giving it responsibility for everything from innovative, entrepreneurial successes to board members' incessant infighting.

For all the power people ascribe to organizational culture, you'd think everyone writing or talking about it would have a clear and deep definition. Yet as we dug into the literature, we found that organizational culture is inherently fuzzy; its foundations are unconscious, invisible, and assumed. Few writers seem to address the full depth of the concept. Consequently, it seems that most of the time, people don't know what they mean when they say "it's the culture." The term is so slippery that it isn't helpful.

As we dug into the literature, we found that organizational culture is inherently fuzzy; its foundations are unconscious, invisible, and assumed. Few writers seem to address the full depth of the concept.

Despite the common references to organizational culture in the nonprofit literature, nonprofit-focused studies in general do not deeply explore what organizational culture is or how to uncover and describe it. Nor do they add to our understanding of organizational culture within the context of nonprofits. Further, if they claim that a relationship between organizational culture and effectiveness does exist, these books and articles do not explain the pathways by which an organization's culture would impact its effectiveness.

We speculate that the wealth of anecdotal references to nonprofit organizational culture and the dearth of empirical research may have two causes. First, "culture" serves as a handy scapegoat to explain inexplicable or uncontrollable organization events. So, for example, nonprofit leaders are apt to say, "That's just part of our organizational culture." Second, the complexity of the topic makes meaningful research costly—especially critical in an environment that is almost always stressed for lack of resources.

Our goal in this book is to deepen your knowledge and appreciation of organizational culture in all its richness and complexity, while enabling you to understand its daily impact on a nonprofit organization's work.

DEFINING ORGANIZATIONAL CULTURE

Let's be very clear from the beginning about what organizational culture means. In general use, culture can be defined as "the totality of socially transmitted behavior patterns, arts, beliefs, institutions, and all other products of human work and characteristics of a community or population" (Kotter and Heskett,

1992, p. 4). Culture, in this definition, is the foundation of a group's fundamental beliefs about the world and the way it operates. Why do human beings create culture? Authors Trice and Beyer (1993) reflect on this question when they write, "Human cultures emerge from people's struggles to manage uncertainties and create some degree of order in social life" (p. 1).

When we talk about organizational culture, we are specifically defining the "community or population" as an organization, in contrast to the entire population of a nation, region, or even an ethnic group. Although we are used to thinking about culture in broad, sweeping terms related to large groups of people, Edgar Schein (1999), one of the preeminent writers and thinkers on the subject, points out that cultures develop "whenever a group has enough common experience" (p. 13). In other words, any group (no matter the size) that is pursuing a task or goal together will ultimately develop a culture. Schein's comment also points to the importance of the early stages of group formation to the creation of the culture.

These groups create culture for the same reasons that all humans do: to manage uncertainty. In the process of managing uncertainty and chaos, people create meaning. They are making sense of their world. This is why so much of the conversation around culture, whether it is national culture or organizational culture, focuses on values and beliefs. Values and beliefs are the "by-products" of humans' quest for meaning and are conveyed through stories. Values and beliefs make the world more understandable by providing guidelines for behavior generally agreed to by the community. As we'll explore in more detail throughout the book, stories are an accessible way to "get at" the real values and beliefs of an organization, and one of the most important stories is the creation story.

We believe the clearest and most actionable definition of organizational culture comes from Schein (2004), who states that organizational culture is "a pattern of basic assumptions—invented, discovered, or developed by a given group as it learns to cope with its problems of external adaptation and internal integration—that has worked well enough to be considered valid and, therefore, to be taught to new members as the correct way to perceive, think, and feel in relation to those problems" (p. 17). Schein goes on to identify three different levels that can be examined in relation to organizational culture: level 1, artifacts, or what people see; level 2, espoused values, or what people say they value; and level 3, underlying assumptions, which answer questions about why artifacts and behaviors are the way they are. This third level is where the "content" and power of organizational culture can be found.

This gives us a start, but in order to tune ourselves into the deep elements of culture, it is helpful to understand more about the content of culture—what to listen for in terms of deep beliefs. In other words, is there a way to narrow down the kinds of beliefs and values that will be most helpful, the kinds of stories to listen for? As Schein (2004) describes, anthropologists have given us guidance in discerning these beliefs, suggesting that we ask penetrating philosophical questions:

Is truth revealed or discovered? In organizations, the question might be, for example, How do you determine the "right" answer to a service, staffing, or quality issue? Imagine the different ways the following nonprofits might answer questions about what kind of service to deliver or about improving quality: RAND Corporation, which uses quantitative and didactic processes; the Aspen Institute, with its Socratic seminars; or a community-based organization crafting an asset-based development plan.

Are humans intrinsically good, evil, or neutral? Can we perfect ourselves, improve, or change? What does it really mean to be human? Think about how and why the most radical elements of Greenpeace might answer these questions of human nature. How about a family counseling service, a fundamentalist Christian organization, or an organization with roots in the military?

How should people interact with one other? Are we cooperative or competitive, individualistic or communal? Are relationships in the office purely professional, or are they friendly and familial? How is conflict handled? How are decisions made? Think of an advocacy organization with a long history of confrontation, in contrast to one that always seems to find a way to collaborate with government agencies. Why are such different approaches used?

As you are looking and listening for the key beliefs at the heart of any organizational culture, pay attention to these deep assumptions about reality (how we know what is true), time (finite or infinite), space (in relation to people or to place), human nature, and human relationships.

More explicitly related to organizations and the content of organizational cultures are the solutions to what organization management researchers call *external survival issues* and *internal integration issues*. External survival refers to how the organization defines itself in relationship to the external world of other organizations, customers, and the operating environment. The way organizations resolve these issues is based on the assumptions an organization makes and is conveyed through mission, strategy, goals, structures, systems and processes, and measurement. In the nonprofit sector, if organizations have identified a theory of change or logic model, they may have surfaced some of these assumptions that answer questions about why they approach their work the way they do. Internal integration is about how the people in the organization relate to one another and is conveyed through common language and concepts, group identity and boundaries, authority and relationships, and the allocation of rewards and status—in other words, assumptions about relationships, teamwork, and decision making. For example, the organization will have special terms and jargon; it will have assumptions about the level of formality or informality expected in interactions with top management.

ACTION

Take a moment to note some of the artifacts and espoused values in your organization or an organization you know well. Don't try to judge or explain them; just describe them. Are there other organizations that would have very similar artifacts? What about values? Can you name another organization with similar espoused values? We suspect you can. Thus it is only as you discover the underlying beliefs—the reason why these values and artifacts exist—that you can see the uniqueness and richness of your organization's culture.

It is, of course, people who make culture. Because culture develops among any group of people, it is clear that everyone is (in this sense) multicultural. Each person has an individual experience, ancestry, and psychology, and each functions in many different cultures. One person may simultaneously carry the Spanish, Native American, Southwestern U.S., American, Methodist, teacher, and academician cultures. All these regional, ethnic, national, historical, religious, local, and professional cultures coexist, and this individual will bring them all to her workplace.

It is also worth noting that in many organizational cultures, particularly cultures that hold together large numbers of people, we see that "Cultures have multiple ideologies; the ideas they express sometimes complement and sometimes contradict each other" (Trice and Beyer, 1993, p. 175). Culture is not monolithic. These contradictions can be disconcerting when you attempt to describe the culture in its entirety. But remember that different aspects of culture develop over time and in response to different challenges. Cultures do not have to be internally consistent.

We are each multicultural, and we each interact individually with many cultures. But there's a mysterious aspect to organizational culture: it exists beyond the reach of any individual and his or her personal multicultural mix. Culture is the "property of" or the "domain of" the group. It is not owned by one person. It is important to keep this in mind as you think about organizational culture, especially in its relation to leadership. Individual employees and leaders inevitably interact with and sometimes influence organizational culture, but the individual's particular cultural makeup is not the culture of the organization. Early in an organization's development, the leader is contributing his or her beliefs and assumptions to the group; if these assumptions about what works and why prove to be successful, they will be taken for granted over time. They will become deeply embedded in the organization's culture. Consequently, although individual beliefs are not the same as group culture, founders have a particularly strong influence over culture. Further, leaders of organizations facing difficult challenges—problems that require the organization to change for its very survival—may also be in a particularly strong position to influence and help evolve organizational culture.

In summary, culture arises when a group faces the inevitable internal needs, external challenges, and uncertainties of existence. It is formed as the group responds to shared experiences, and is the domain of the group rather than the individual. It is both the behavior and the reason for the behavior. In fact, when you talk about organizational culture, the reason for behaviors is paramount.

WHY DO NONPROFITS EXIST?

With this perspective on what organizational culture is and what kinds of assumptions make up the heart of culture, we'll take a brief look at the literature on the history, laws, and theory behind the existence of nonprofit organizations in the United States. As you will see, we believe that the politics, economics, laws, and procedures that permit the existence of nonprofit organizations result in certain underlying values that are typically associated with nonprofits. These are important because the broad strokes that show up in these theories and mandates shape the context in which each individual nonprofit develops its culture. These traits give you an idea of *what kinds of things to look and listen for* as you try to describe a nonprofit's culture.

Economic Theories

Several economic theories have been posed to explain the existence of nonprofit organizations (Hansmann, 1987). At their essence, most of these theories cite some form of market failure—goods or services are not being provided because they cost so much that few people of any means can afford them without subsidy (for example, art productions), people are experiencing difficulties with trust or information (see our discussion of contract failure), customers have little money (for example, low-income housing), or there is no identifiable customer (for example, the environment). For our purposes here, we are interested in two economic theories: provision of public good theory[1] and contract failure theory.

Provision of public good theory suggests that nonprofit organizations come into being to meet individual wants and needs that are not being met by the government or private business. In theory, government has an incentive to offer public goods provided at the level desired by the "median voter." Some people want a greater amount or slightly different version of this public good, so a nonprofit arises to provide this public good or service. The organization takes a nonprofit form because the for-profit sector does not have an effective way to deal with the problem of people who benefit from the service without paying for it ("free riders") and, therefore, cannot capture sufficient revenue. Think about public radio, the American Heart Association, or March of Dimes. We suggest that nonprofits fitting this economic theory will have deep beliefs about equity, fairness, and access to service.

Contract failure theory postulates that nonprofits are likely to arise in areas where the consumer is unable to judge the quantity or quality of a good or service. According to this theory, this asymmetry of information makes it more likely that consumers would trust a "seller" that has an altruistic motive rather than a profit motive—that is, a nonprofit. For example, it may be difficult to judge the quality of a day-care provider or services to Alzheimer's patients. According to this theory, consumers (parents or children) would feel more comfortable purchasing services from a nonprofit, and, consequently, nonprofits have a competitive advantage in offering these services. This theory assumes a deep level of trust on the part of the consumer. It helps explain why the values of openness, transparency, and accountability seem to be strongly embedded in nonprofits. Further, this theory sheds light on why nonprofits often distrust the market and competition as fair means of resource distribution.

Political Theories

A number of political theories have been created to explain the existence of nonprofit organizations in terms of both the public participation they facilitate and political history (Douglas, 1987). The political theories surrounding nonprofit organizations are relatively complex. For our purposes, we are interested in the following three: civic diversity theory, general participation theory, and innovation theory.

Civic diversity theory argues that nonprofit organizations arise as a means and mechanism for allowing greater, more diverse participation in public life. The "central paradox of democracy is that the people are sovereign but many; there is not one will of the people but several sometimes contradictory wills. . . . [Nonprofits present] a mechanism through which conflicts of values, interests and views can, if not be resolved, be at least accommodated" (Douglas, 1987, p. 47). This theory does a good job of explaining the existence of such advocacy organizations as Greenpeace or the NAACP. Nonprofits arising most explicitly out of this need are particularly likely to have strong beliefs around diversity, tolerance, and the role of these in the public debate. Interestingly, however, these beliefs do not mean that diversity *within* the organization is always valued. For example, the mandate of an organization engaged in public life may mean that it is more important that the group speak with a single voice and that the organization not accept diverse views or people.

General participation theory is based in part on political history and in part on theories about the mediating role played by civil society. This theory captures the historical experience of the United States as the first democracy. You may be familiar with this theory from Tocqueville's essay on the American penchant for voluntary organizing. This reflects a sense that individuals are morally obligated to participate in voluntary efforts and that such volunteering is best accomplished through civic association.

A related idea is that independent organizations have a role as mediating structures between private and public life.[2] In this role, nonprofits are thought to be the best vehicles for empowering people to advocate for policy change and for providing social and civic interaction outside the realm of government. This theory accounts for a wide range of nonprofits, from social and civic organizations such as the Boy Scouts to membership associations of professionals. Nonprofits arising most explicitly out of the needs described in general participation theory are likely to believe strongly that participation is important; they will have rules around participation and assume there's a need for mechanisms to ensure adequate participation in decision making. Further, they are likely to have traditions that include volunteers providing services.

Innovation theory explains nonprofits as arising from the public's need for new services and products and the government's inability to act on this need until there is some certainty around the approach. "Before a democratic government can embark on any course of action, the case for it must be accepted by a relatively large section of the population. . . . if the approach has already been tried by a voluntary body and proved viable, government can then follow using the experience and evidence gained by the voluntary organizations" (Douglas, 1987, p. 48). A subset of innovation theory is the idea that nonprofits arise to offer greater flexibility in the provision of public services. Democratic governments must treat their citizens equally; they are constrained by values of equality and justice. Consequently, they must provide the same services to all. Further, their bureaucratic nature restricts the provision of services. This does not mean that nonprofits do not have their own bureaucracies, but they are generally freer than governments. Examples of nonprofits fitting nicely into this theory include operating foundations, many community development corporations, and economic development districts that take a nonprofit form. Nonprofits arising from this need are likely to have particularly close relationships with government and strong values around research, trying new ideas, and being more flexible than their government counterparts. They are likely to struggle with the balance in their interactions with government and end up in contradictory conversations around their ability to innovate and be flexible in relation to their desire to have efficient processes that allow them to serve more people.

Legal Mandates

In practice, the primary legal mandate that distinguishes nonprofit organizations from private business is the *nondistribution constraint:* nonprofit organizations can only retain and distribute revenue and assets for specified organizational purposes. Nonprofit organizations (like all corporations) must be governed by boards of directors; the directors' legal duties vary by state, but usually include a duty of obedience to the organization's mission. The duty of obedience to mission is somewhat different from the duties of directors of for-profit businesses. An additional difference is that traditionally board members of nonprofits are volunteers. There are many IRS categories for nonprofit organizations. For 501 (c)(3) organizations, their purpose must be charitable. In some ways, legal and procedural requirements are expressions of the political and economic theories about why nonprofits exist, and further distinguish nonprofits from business and government (Oleck, 1988).

The echoes of economic theories about the existence of nonprofits are seen in the nondistribution constraint. A nonprofit organization's net proceeds cannot be distributed among members or owners. An underlying idea here is that a nonprofit organization is not driven by the goal of maximizing the financial bottom line and, instead, focuses on quality or on serving more people. (A similar concept was expressed in the contract failure theory; nonprofits are trustworthy because they are not profit driven.) In many organizations, this emphasis on quality and quantity has led to the placing of heightened value on the professional opinion of the staff providing services or running programs. In such nonprofits, conversations and behavior focus on how to improve the quality or quantity of services. On the level of organizational culture, this means many nonprofits will have chosen early in their lives to focus on quality and quantity, and the behaviors based on this decision are likely to be deeply ingrained. A corollary is that such organizations will focus energy on the mission or cause rather than on profit (or surplus revenue). Therefore, successes for the organization are likely to be related to its causes, and the beliefs and behaviors that led to these successes are likely to be deeply embedded in the organization.

A second legal mandate can be found in the tradition of voluntary governance and the often legally required duty of obedience. Voluntary governance is based on two fundamental ideas: (1) voluntary action is intrinsically good and a relevant way to approach social needs, and (2) oversight by a group of volunteers will hold the organization accountable to the public. These twin ideas have led to an emphasis on altruism, including altruistic motivations and visions on the part of staff and, sometimes, a focus on participation and participatory processes that can be time-consuming and costly. In many cases, the emphasis on volunteerism and altruism leads nonprofit organizations to assume that staff should work for lower salaries than they would earn in other sectors; there is a role for volunteers and a lack of comfort with business language and concepts that measure success in dollars.

The final legal mandate for 501(c)(3)s is that their purposes must be charitable. The underlying idea for 501(c)(3)s is that favorable tax status is warranted if the organization is serving a charitable (public) purpose. The definition of *charitable* has a long political history in the United States; for our purposes, it means serving the public, providing a public good, or assisting government in delivering its services. The charitable purpose requirement adds little new to the context of organizational culture, but it highlights the focus on altruism and the common expectation that nonprofit staff should be motivated by altruistic concerns. Ultimately, the service or program is important, whereas administration and infrastructure are not.

The nature of nonprofit organizations' existence as expressed through their economic, political, legal, and historical evolution suggests that there are key values with which most nonprofits will have grappled in their creation and growth. These values are likely to be present in some form in most nonprofits, and they may function as a "skeleton" on which to hang a comprehensive description of their organizational culture.[3] Keep in mind that the list of values themselves does not describe a particular organization's culture. To flesh out the description of any organization's culture, we must look at how those values were established and the behaviors that have resulted.

The nature of nonprofit organizations'
existence as expressed through their economic,
political, legal, and historical evolution suggests that
there are key values with which most nonprofits will
have grappled in their creation and growth.

Table 1.1 summarizes the theories about the existence of nonprofit organizations. It further shows how those theories are reflected through values that tend to be shared across the nonprofit sector.

Table 1.1
Nonprofit Theories and Values

General Theory About the Existence of the Nonprofit Sector	Values That May Inform Deep Assumptions in Nonprofit Organizations
Provision of Public Good The nonprofit form addresses the free rider problem.	Equity, fairness, and access to services.
Contract Failure Theory The nonprofit form has a competitive advantage because of the information inequity in the service.	Openness, transparency, and accountability. Sometimes there is a general underlying distrust of the market and competition, and deep skepticism that a competitive market will lead to the best allocation of resources.

Civic Diversity Theory

The nonprofit exists to allow more voices to be heard than can be accommodated by decisions of government.

Citizens' importance in playing a role in the public debate, including diversity and tolerance. In some cases, the assumption is that diversity is good; in others, the idea of solidarity of a single voice will be more important than encouraging diversity per se. In both cases, notice that the organization has to struggle with what it believes is appropriate with regard to diversity and tolerance.

Innovation Theory

Nonprofits rise from the public's need for new services and products and the government's inability to act on this need until there is some certainty around the approach.

Research, trying new ideas, and flexibility (as compared to government bureaucracy). Close relationships with government may cause contradictory conversations around the nonprofit's ability to innovate and be flexible and its desire to have efficient processes that allow it to serve more people.

General Participation Theory

The nonprofit plays a mediating role between individual interests and societal interests.

Broad participation and volunteerism. The nonprofit's rules are likely to require community or membership participation in the governance and decision making of the organization.

Legal Constraints

Nondistribution constraint

Focus on quality and quantity as part of the approach to the work and a driving motivation behind what to do with additional resources. Definitions of success are often closely related to clients—people, animals, or causes.

Voluntary governance

Altruism, volunteerism, and discomfort with business language.

501(c)(3)s and charitable purposes

Altruism particularly as part of staff motivation; lack of concern or interest in administration and infrastructure.

CONTEMPORARY INFLUENCES ON NONPROFIT CULTURE

In addition to the political, economic, and legal contexts that support the existence of a broad nonprofit culture, there are contemporary forces at work. The American nonprofit sector continues to evolve, bringing new experiences that influence and shift its culture. Some of the most prominent influences impacting the sector today are discussed in the next sections.

Private Sector Practices

Since the mid-1980s, nonprofits have had considerable interest in learning about private sector business management. Paul Light, a nonprofit scholar, notes that in the private sector there is often an underlying belief that the market can best allocate resources, that competition inevitably yields efficiency, and that a focus on finances is the best measure of success. As previously noted, nonprofits often have an underlying distrust of the market. However, this traditional distrust is being challenged today with the rise of social enterprise, low-profit corporate forms, and the idea that social venture capital is a valid alternative way to fund nonprofit organizations. These experiments at the edge of the traditional nonprofit business model are confronting long-held assumptions in the nonprofit sector about its role, what makes it unique, and the value of fiscal measures of success. With an organizational culture lens and an understanding of the legal, theoretical, and historical origins of nonprofits, you can see the root of tension as people from for-profit businesses bring new ideas to nonprofits.

Noting a less extreme form of this trend, Peter Brinckerhoff, an author and consultant on nonprofit management, talks about the need for non-profits to say no to opportunities that will stretch the organization too thin. A productive organizational culture must balance mission and fundraising functions. Brinckerhoff puts it this way: "Mission . . . mission . . . mission— but no money, no mission. Nonprofits must say 'no' if there isn't enough money." The successes and failures of these experiments with a more "busi-nesslike" mentality will shape the organizational culture of nonprofits that engage in them.

The successes and failures of these experiments with a more "businesslike" mentality will shape the organizational culture of nonprofits that engage in them.

The Internet as an Organizing and Networking Tool

The increasing role of the Internet in organizing and managing social networks has challenged nonprofits whose fundamental beliefs about participation assume face-to-face interaction. The success of President Obama's campaign using these tools, and the growth of Facebook, Twitter, LinkedIn, YouTube, and so on are examples of how technology is creating new context for nonprofits. As organizations without Facebook fans or Twitter followers get left behind, new technologies are pushing on assumptions about how nonprofits should effectively organize and sustain participation. One of the thought leaders we interviewed, Ruth McCambridge, a longtime capacity builder in the field and the editor of *Nonprofit Quarterly*, stated,

> I think there are significant and deep changes in the external environment and structural changes that are happening in the nonprofit sector. As the hierarchical structures of the industrial age give way to the looser forms of the information age, we are seeing it impact

organization structure—via the rise of networks. We are finding that we have to function largely as networks or in networks. That is very different from stand-alone organizations. This is impacting culture and characteristics of culture that are successful. . . . Young people are more likely to explore these new forms. I'm humbled with their ease at using technology to create effective networks. These changes should be welcomed. They are going to happen.

Sweeping Leadership Change

Members of the baby-boom generation have profoundly influenced the creation of many nonprofits, and now they are beginning to retire or move into second careers. The nonprofit sector is in the midst of the largest wave of leadership change in its history. New leaders carry with them a different set of generational experiences. They are unattached to the experiences and experiments of the 1960s and 1970s and less wary of the role of business in solving social problems. After all, they have Patagonia and Ben and Jerry's as examples of socially involved, mission-driven businesses. They have also participated in nonprofit organizations while meeting their service learning requirements in high school and engaging in alternative spring break experiences in college. They want balance between their work and personal lives; they are tech-savvy and more comfortable with distributed leadership. As they come to leadership positions and move onto boards of directors, there will be an inevitable evolution of nonprofit organizational cultures.

Increasing Professionalism

The trend toward professionalism in the nonprofit sector, which has its roots in various academic traditions, is reaching a new phase. Early leaders of nonprofit organizations generally came out of community organizing, social work, or direct program delivery. Today, there are more than two hundred nonprofit management degree granting programs (Hall, 2007) and an uncounted number of certificate programs that highlight the importance of management and leadership skills. Brinckerhoff notes, for example, that a "new generation of health care managers have management training but have not worked in health care delivery, and that is shifting the organizational culture of health care away from the focus on patient care." In other fields, the shift may be less stark, but as those with professional training in management and leadership increasingly enter nonprofit organizations, they will certainly confront deep beliefs around the intrinsic good of volunteerism and the nature of charity.

IMPACT OF INDIVIDUAL LEADERS

There is one final element about the "nature" of nonprofits that has particular consequences for organizational culture and is seen across the nonprofit sector. Much of the literature (and certainly our interviews with thought leaders) point to the importance of leadership in the formation, management, and intentional shifting of organizational culture. Most nonprofits are small organizations, and leaders play a particularly powerful role in staffing and in shaping the culture. The commonality across the sector here is not reflected in a particular value, but in the assumption that the leader is critical to organizational success. Among small and start-up nonprofits, leaders, particularly founding leaders, have succeeded by convincing donors and other funders to give them resources. They gain these resources by generating a sense of importance and passion for the cause the organization addresses and the service it provides. Because of this particularly strong role that many leaders, especially founding leaders, play in nonprofits, we suspect they may have an even stronger influence over the formation of organizational culture than leaders in for-profit businesses.

A SPECIAL SUBSET: COMMUNITY-BASED
SERVICE NONPROFITS

We believe many community-based nonprofit organizations share an overarching subsector culture, which, like the skeleton of the larger nonprofit sector culture, was created through the unique circumstances at their inception. Through this example, we're also considering how some of the common values of nonprofits explored earlier interact with the environment at the time of founding to influence a whole subset of nonprofits.

The shared culture of community-based service nonprofits was predominantly formed in the 1960s and 1970s. The federal War on Poverty began funneling money directly to communities. As a result, new organizations were formed with an explicit set of underlying guidelines about community empowerment, engagement, and the strength of community organizing to eradicate poverty. These new organizations, called community development and community action agencies, were heavily influenced by the experiences of organized labor and by Saul Alinsky, the Chicago-based organizer often considered the father of community organizing. Alinsky's book *Rules for Radicals* (1971) became a seminal text for a generation of community organizations and organizers. At the same time, the civil rights and antiwar movements were capturing the imaginations of many in a new generation. Young baby boomers were riding freedom buses in the South and helping organize voter registration. Money became available for these new community-based organizations at a time when no one had any real experience running these kinds of community agencies, so young baby boomers got the jobs. Thus, in the 1960s and 1970s, new organizations were formed and led by a generation whose life experiences to that point focused on values of equity, social justice, fairness, participation, and opportunity. They incorporated these values into the cultures of the organizations they were creating.

This confluence of historical change, federal money, and a large generation of young leaders created a unique subsector culture among these nonprofits. The values at the heart of these community-based service and development organizations include the following:

A hero mentality. The organizations were founded with an attitude that "we can make a difference in people's lives if we all work hard enough." In many cases, this led to a hero mentality that values long hours, low pay (so that more money can go to services), and "saving" those in need. Here we see the incorporation of nonprofit values of access to services, equity, and quantity of services that are predicted by public good theory and the nondistribution constraint.

Ambiguous relationships with primary government funders. These organizations operated with the notion that they could and should work in collaboration with government and government resources, but they also felt that being "of the community" would make them more innovative and flexible. In many cases, these organizations were created through a partnership with federal agencies and federal funding, but wanted local control—an inherently tense situation. So although organizations valued government and believed it had a role to play, particularly in funding, they also were strongly committed to their communities and to the flexible solutions that could come with local control. This complex relationship with government and sometimes ambiguous relationship with primary government funders are classic manifestations of the values and tensions that innovation theory predicts.

Community-driven, participatory processes. The community organizing background fostered a sense that the organizations needed to go beyond merely providing services *to* communities to creating services *with* communities. Although processes for community participation take more time and raise other issues of what today we call cultural competency, ultimately these organizations believe that community participation is a critical part of creating change. This value often leads to a strong commitment to ensuring that there are ways for those receiving services to participate in the organization. (Whether or not these are effective or appropriate from the viewpoint of those receiving services is a different question. In fact, in many cases, the early founders and staff of these organizations included people from outside the community who had good intentions but may have had a different worldview than the members of the community they were serving.) So in these organizations we see values and beliefs about participation, community empowerment, and pathways to economic success.

A focus on racial justice. Racial justice, which at that time focused primarily around the experience of black and white Americans, was a predominant theme in 1960s and 1970s. Any community-based organization formed at this time was likely to have strong assumptions and beliefs around race and the role of integration. In general, these assumptions were likely to fall into two categories. Either they assumed that a diverse staff and broad engagements (integration) across racial boundaries were the right way to address community issues, civil rights, and economic opportunity, or they assumed that blacks from poor communities needed to be in control of organizations—needed to "own or create" their own power—and that participation by whites in such organizations might be harmful. The legacy of the racial struggles and of the solutions organizations came up with during the turbulence of the 1960s and 1970s is still seen today in many organizations. This legacy is also an example of the tensions at which civic diversity theory hints.

Other nonprofit subsector cultures undoubtedly exist, based on regulations that govern them, the organizations' primary focus, and numerous other factors. We present the previous example because this particular subsector is prevalent, well known, and illustrative. It's a good illustration of how our broader conclusions about the evolution of a shared nonprofit culture work at the subsector level.

ACTION

When was your organization formed? What were the major socioeconomic and political trends at the time? Where do you see echoes of those in your organization and the way it solves survival challenges and resolves differences about how change happens? How do they manifest themselves?

OUR VIEW OF NONPROFIT ORGANIZATIONAL CULTURE

We like the popular analogy of organizational culture as an iceberg (Kotter and Rathgeber, 2006). As shown in Figure 1.1, the tip is made of the visible artifacts of the organization and its espoused values. These include such things as the way one is welcomed at the organization, who sits in which offices, the kinds of processes managers use, and so forth.

However, the iceberg's foundation, its most stable and critical part, is hidden underwater. Similarly, most of organizational culture resides beneath the surface of awareness, yet this hidden part is the most stable. If you want to know what the iceberg looks like and what it's made of, you're going to need to don

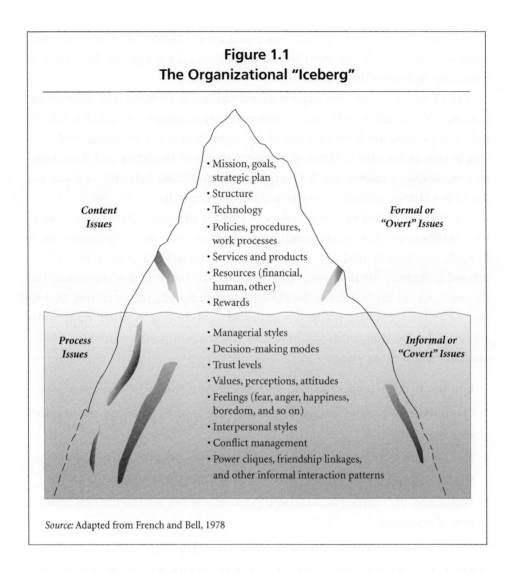

Figure 1.1
The Organizational "Iceberg"

Content Issues

- Mission, goals, strategic plan
- Structure
- Technology
- Policies, procedures, work processes
- Services and products
- Resources (financial, human, other)
- Rewards

Formal or "Overt" Issues

Process Issues

- Managerial styles
- Decision-making modes
- Trust levels
- Values, perceptions, attitudes
- Feelings (fear, anger, happiness, boredom, and so on)
- Interpersonal styles
- Conflict management
- Power cliques, friendship linkages, and other informal interaction patterns

Informal or "Covert" Issues

Source: Adapted from French and Bell, 1978

scuba gear, get out the sonar, take core samples, and work mightily to deduce what elements constitute its hidden foundation. Even then, your picture of the iceberg will be limited—you can sketch its boundaries and tell something about its internal makeup, but you'll never know the whole thing.

Discerning the constitution of organizational culture requires similar effort. How do you determine the true shape of the foundation by looking at its tip? How do you ask about something of which people are generally unaware? How do you take "core samples" of the culture and generalize them to the whole? How do you make predictions based on the limited information from those samples? And if you want to move the cultural iceberg, just how large a leadership tugboat will you require?

The literature shows that organizational culture is complex and difficult to change. This conflicts with many contemporary management articles, which hold out promise for fairly easy use of (or management of) organizational culture in change initiatives. Although we agree that understanding and describing an organization's culture can help explain organizational behavior and can be useful in a change initiative, there is nothing easy about it.

Our own work and extensive review of existing literature allow us to make a few contributions to the understanding of organizational culture in nonprofits.

First, we did not find any evidence that organizational culture should be defined differently for nonprofits than it is for any other type of organization. As noted, we do think there is the skeleton of a nonprofit sector culture that is created by the economic, political, social, and legal context in which nonprofits are formed. Most nonprofits will have underlying assumptions related to at least some of the following values:

- Equity and fairness are critical in the way that people deal with one another.

- It is important to hold specific discussions about who can access services, for how long, and why.

- Trust is critical to success in making the changes we want to see happen in the world, so we'll operate in ways that are open, transparent and accountable.

- Sometimes the marketplace and competition will not lead to the best allocation of resources.

- Citizens should play a role in public debate and civic life.

- Diversity and tolerance are important values, and we need to determine how to handle diversity and tolerance within the context of our mission. (As a corollary: at times, solidarity and diversity are not in alignment, and we will need to choose one or the other.)

- Applied research, new and experimental ideas, innovation, and flexibility are valuable differences between nonprofits and our government counterparts. The way to find truth is through various means of "trying things out."

- Sometimes there is internal conflict between the need to be flexible and innovative and the need to have the efficient but uniform processes that will help us serve more people. These conflicts may become more noticeable when we work closely with government counterparts.

- Broad participation is important, so our "rules" should require community or membership participation in the governance and decision making of the organization.
- Volunteerism is important; it is often how we got our start.
- Quality and quantity are part of our approach to our work and a driving motivation behind what we decide to do with additional or surplus resources.
- Our organizational success is closely related to success for our clients or causes.
- Altruism is a key to staff motivation; a corollary is that administration and infrastructure are not highly valued.

We also believe there are elements of organizational culture that are likely to be held across particular large classes or types of nonprofit organizations. Any group with enough common experience can form its own culture. Fields or categories of nonprofits, as in the example of community-based nonprofits discussed earlier in this chapter, are more likely to share more specific cultural elements when they are formed at similar times under similar sociopolitical and economic influences.

Another interesting phenomenon that appears frequently in the nonprofit sector is that the people served or the program participants influence the organizational culture. Nonprofit staff and sometimes board members often relate closely to the behavior and needs of the people they are serving. In many cases, there are current or former clients on the board or working for the organization. By itself, this is simply reflective of the nonprofit sector culture, which values participation and empowerment. However, in some organizations, this foundational belief is stretched, and the organization begins to take on elements of its client's dysfunctional behaviors.

For example, Carol Lukas and Ruth McCambridge, nonprofit thought leaders, noted that an unproductive culture arises when organizations take on the symptoms or behavior of people they are serving—especially "victim behavior." They noted seeing this with organizations serving battered women, crime victims, and people living in poverty. This negatively impacts the organization's ability to obtain funding and be effective with others who do not share their viewpoint or perspective. For example, the victim mentality might reflect the following kinds of beliefs: "Those in power are always out to get us," "We need to be strong and stand up to them, but we are weak and can't do that," or "We're too small to affect that." If an organization acts from these kinds of beliefs, it will have difficulty forming strong partnerships with other agencies and making bold decisions, and may even lash out at those who could otherwise help it, such as strong and successful businesses.

A final note of caution about organizational culture. Because people use the term so loosely, we also think it is helpful to state what organizational culture is not. Organizational culture is not

- The processes of an organization, a philosophical statement such as mission, or the theoretical underpinnings of a service delivery approach
- The tools of management, such as appreciative inquiry or social enterprise
- Organizational climate
- The structure or reporting relationships
- The way people talk to (or e-mail) one another
- The way one is welcomed by the CEO or a secretary
- Who is in what office
- What the leader says is important
- What the strategic plan says are core values
- Rules for getting along

Please note, however, that all these things are strongly affected by organizational culture. We see organizational culture as "a pattern of beliefs" and "basic assumptions" (Schein, 2004, p. 12). This means that these beliefs and basic assumptions manifest themselves over and over again throughout the organization. These assumptions have worked well enough over time in addressing problems the organization faced that they are taught to newcomers. For us, organizational culture is inalterably bound to the solutions to challenges, issues, or questions—particularly those solutions formed early on in the organization's life or during times of challenge and crisis.

Organizational culture is inalterably bound to the solutions to challenges, issues, or questions—particularly those solutions formed early on in the organization's life or during times of challenge and crisis.

Organizational culture is a big container. It can refer to both "the whole" of the organization's culture (all the artifacts, values, and underlying assumptions) and to whatever aspect of that big container we are discussing at the moment (that is, "We have deep assumptions around teamwork" or "Our practice is research based and results driven"). When using the term to refer to a particular slice of culture, keep in mind that organizational culture is also an integrated whole. Although you may uncover and push on parts of the culture, you don't know what unintended consequences such pressure will bring.

Six Examples of Nonprofit Culture in Action

At this point, we hope you are becoming convinced that organizational culture is real and that there are some predictable trends across all nonprofits. In this chapter, we use stories from a mix of nonprofit organizations to illustrate the ways in which an observer can use elements of an organization's deep, underlying assumptions.

The stories staff members tell—the narratives of an organization—often shed light on the deeper aspects of organizational culture. And stress in an organization helps bring to the surface otherwise hidden aspects of culture. Think of it this way: as waves of change rock the iceberg of culture, its base tips up and we can, for a moment, see more of it, as shown in Figure 2.1. Another way of thinking about this is that stress places pressure on the basic foundational assumptions and values that motivate (or justify) behavior in the organization, thus baring them for easier examination.

With one exception, our resources enabled us to conduct one interview with each organization, which we believe surfaced enough to illustrate the observations we are making about organizational culture. These interviews also served as the foundation for the deeper Revealing Organizational Culture (ROC) process we review in the next chapter.

The literature on nonprofit management has identified many typical nonprofit stressors. With a general knowledge of those stressors as a backdrop, we

33

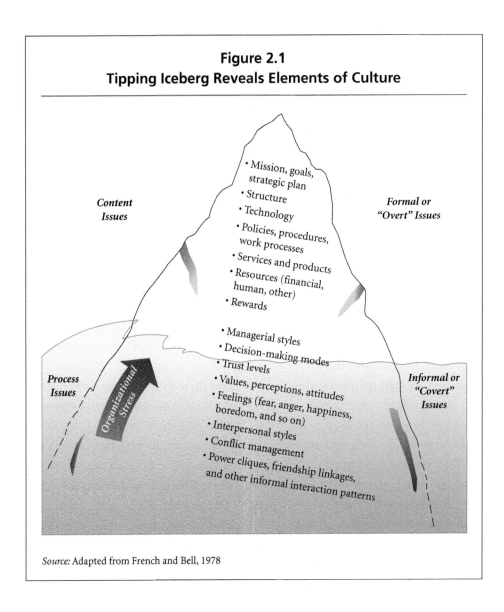

Figure 2.1
Tipping Iceberg Reveals Elements of Culture

Content Issues

Formal or "Overt" Issues

- Mission, goals, strategic plan
- Structure
- Technology
- Policies, procedures, work processes
- Services and products
- Resources (financial, human, other)
- Rewards

Organizational Stress

- Managerial styles
- Decision-making modes
- Trust levels
- Values, perceptions, attitudes
- Feelings (fear, anger, happiness, boredom, and so on)
- Interpersonal styles
- Conflict management
- Power cliques, friendship linkages, and other informal interaction patterns

Process Issues

Informal or "Covert" Issues

Source: Adapted from French and Bell, 1978

selected organizations that had undergone one or more of the following challenges in recent years:

Life cycle change—evolving into a more mature organization

Executive Director transition—change in leadership

External change—change in operating environment

We ultimately selected two representative organizations for each of the stress situations listed here. We are deeply grateful to the organizations and individuals who shared their stories.

ORGANIZATIONAL LIFE CYCLE SHIFT

According to organizational life cycle theory, organizations, like human beings, go through fairly predictable stages of growth and change, and the challenges and systems most likely to be effective during those stages are also somewhat predictable (Stevens, 2002). There have been many different ways of dividing the stages of an organization's life cycle, but they typically differentiate between the start-up phase and the next "maturing" phase. Usually, this transition includes a change in the type of leadership from a single, dominant founder to more shared leadership. This transition also includes the development of systems and procedures.

In this section, we look at two organizations that in some ways were evolving (or were trying to evolve) from start-up to a more mature phase. We note that, as life cycle theory would predict, organizational cultural elements around leadership and the types of systems and processes that are most effective surface during this time.

Arctusis: Aspiring Beyond a Founder

Arctusis is a membership and support organization for women who suffer from a chronic, painful disease. Besides supporting women and their loved ones, Arctusis advocates on their behalf with the medical establishment, which historically has neglected and discounted the disorder. *Note:* The name and certain details have been changed to disguise the organization described in this case. Our informant in this case was able to give much greater detail than was possible in others. We've tried to pare down the information to be most relevant, but it is still somewhat longer than other stories.

History Arctusis began as a grassroots entity and has been run by the founding executive for nearly three decades. She is a passionate, persistent woman who suffers from the painful disease and speaks about it in a compelling way. She takes great pride in having changed the medical establishment's understanding of the disease. Where once the establishment did not even believe the disorder existed, the founder's efforts have changed medical practice.

Physicians now understand the symptoms, diagnose the disease, and prescribe appropriately. Initially a lone cry in the wilderness, the founder for years showed up to make her case at what seemed like every medical conference around the world.

For the first ten years, the founder–executive director ran the organization out of her home, calling on volunteer support from those touched by the disease. She described the early years as a struggle to get the medical establishment to believe that women's experiences were valid and as important as a doctor's medical credentials. Her forceful personality was a key to the organization's success for many years. Without it, the organization would not have been created, let alone had a significant impact on many lives.

Challenge In 2006, the Arctusis board began investigating several trends: high staff turnover, substantial decline in membership, and competition with other organizations. It became clear that the executive director was stifling the creativity and innovation of other staff members while lessening the impact of the organization's work. Moreover, membership had declined from over nine thousand to approximately three thousand during the past decade, a powerful vote of dissatisfaction by the recipients of its services. Some of these members had split from the organization to create another with a similar mission.

In lengthy discussions over the course of months, the board decided that the organization needed new executive leadership if it were to continue to develop and grow. After failing to reach an agreement that would have created a new role for the founding executive director, the board terminated her. However, the meeting where the vote took place lacked a quorum, and the deposed executive director was able to get a court to void the board's action. Based on the court's order, the board was dismissed, and the organization's membership voted for a new board that in turn reinstated the founding executive.

Some members of the board continued efforts to resolve the organization's problems. Meanwhile, staff members described the environment as chaotic and uncoordinated. Their greatest complaint was the executive's attempts to control every aspect of their work. Many staff members said they were not allowed to do jobs they were hired to do; she discouraged any initiative on their part. Moreover, the executive director discouraged communication among staff members. There were no conference rooms for meetings out of her hearing range. Staff meetings were characterized by one-way communication from the executive director with little opportunity for meaningful input from staff. Interestingly, operations staff were physically separated (working a floor apart) from the executive and program staff, who worked together, creating further communication barriers.

The executive resisted efforts to change these patterns, even when a consultant was brought in to help. In the consultant's words, the executive seemed to feel threatened by proposed changes that appeared to empower other staff members, and went into "fight" mode. The executive persisted in a pattern of quickly firing staff not viewed by her as sufficiently compliant. As one staff member put it, "[The executive director] believes it's 'my way or the highway.' I have to accept this if I want to keep my job." As of late 2007, despite the efforts of an organization development consultant and the desire of the staff, the organization had made only limited changes in operating systems, governance, and staff responsibilities that would constitute a progression to the next stage of the organization's development—and, all hoped, reverse its recent declines.

Although staff members wanted very much to make changes that would bring new levels of efficiency, effectiveness, and empowerment, the executive director's forceful personality prevented many of these changes from taking place. This may have been because she perceived them as banging against some of the core elements of individuality, fighting, and persistence that characterized the success of the organization in its start-up phase. The executive director continued to believe that only she knew what was best for the organization. And although this attitude was clearly responsible for the organization's creation and initial impact, it was now stifling the organization and the people within it. As one staff member declared, "[The founder's] once beautiful garden is turning brown and dying."

Culture   This founding executive was facing challenges that often accompany social entrepreneurs who rebel against systems. However, there were clear elements of organizational culture at play as well. In this case, the founder's values, approaches, and successes during the first two decades of the organization's life had become the organization's underlying belief system. She had worked to maintain that system even as it showed diminishing and negative returns.

Changes in structure that would allow more cross-communication and more independence among staff were undoubtedly running against the founder's deeply held (and likely unconscious) rebellion against the establishment. It is possible that the physical separation of operations staff and program staff was a manifestation of the assumption that all "establishment" is "bad": operations are a necessity of bureaucracy, and bureaucracy is what creates establishment.

Further, the founder's success through persistence and fighting was folded into the organization as a cultural assumption that this was the best way to accomplish goals. It reappeared as her forcing her will on staff and speedily terminating the noncompliant.

In these cultural artifacts, you can clearly see that culture is created through an organization's early successes. We think this story also reveals something that may be more typical of nonprofits than for-profit businesses, which almost always start small and stay small for years before growing: the founder has an outsized influence on the organization's culture. This founder succeeded by fighting the establishment, through persistence and deep confidence in her decisions and perceptions. In fact, the employee's comment about it being the founder's way or the highway is an expression of exactly what made the organization succeed for many years: sheer force of will. The organizational patterns that now appeared to be holding the organization back were established and reinforced during years of success.

This story is a good example of the interplay between leadership and organizational culture. The deepest current in this organization's culture was the heavy influence of the founding executive's experiences, drive, and values. Her early struggles and successes sowed the seeds of several fundamental beliefs in the organizational culture:

1. Women should be empowered to take charge of their own health care and well-being.

2. The medical establishment cannot be trusted to provide the right care and treatment for women, especially women with this disease; by corollary, establishments cannot be trusted.

3. Persistence and the power of individual experiences and stories are valid and will be effective through a *singular* strong voice. (Advocacy by many different voices has been less supported through the organization's history.)

4. Peer support is important.

5. Rights need to be fought for.

6. Sufferers of the disorder are underdogs—underresourced and unlikely challengers—in this fight.

Taken together, the first two beliefs lead to an organizational culture that disdains "establishment" and its requisite bureaucracy. One can also observe tension between the roles of being supportive and of fighting persistently; the organization had provided and endorsed peer support, but had succeeded by being a tough place that fought for recognition, education, and research.

Further Considerations and Reflections   Arctusis's culture says that one person makes a difference. It also says that one person knows what's best—whether it be an individual with a disease that is not recognized by the medical establishment or an executive director operating with a set of beliefs different from that of the organization's board of directors or staff members. The story makes clear how these cultural beliefs eventually thwarted the organization's development. There may be ways in which a change agent could use the same beliefs to support change. However, the culture also supported strong leadership, and change would therefore likely require the same kind of strong, willful leadership that the current executive reflected. Unfortunately, that kind of leadership was unlikely to develop under the current executive and board. An exceptionally strong and savvy board leader would need to emerge and assert the board's authority in the face of resistance from the executive director.

The organization development consultant who worked on this case noted that some limited successes occurred when the executive was presented a series of options from which she might choose. However, that change path would still require leadership from somewhere offering the choices to the executive. Taken together, the changes in the environment (in part due to Arctusis's success in changing the medical establishment) and the inability of executive leadership to change suggest that the likely path for this organization is a continued decline and potential closing of its doors.

Questions

1. What would this organization look like had it been founded by a collective rather than an individual?

2. What would have happened had the board that terminated the executive director been more careful about quorum?

Somos Mayfair: Becoming Its Own Organization

Somos Mayfair is a community-based organization located in the economically poor and predominately immigrant neighborhood of Mayfair in east San Jose, California. Somos Mayfair serves a community of about twenty thousand. The community has a long history of homegrown leaders. Many active Latino political leaders have their roots in Mayfair, and Cesar Chavez began his organizing work there.

History Somos Mayfair began life in 1997 as the Mayfair Improvement Initiative. In 1996, the William and Flora Hewlett Foundation began a neighborhood improvement initiative and selected Mayfair as the first site to test out its idea of conducting comprehensive community improvement efforts (a then-new process now called a *comprehensive community initiative*, which sought to address problems in an integrated, comprehensive way, led by those in the community). The foundation chose the Mayfair community because its struggles with poverty and allied issues were shared by many poor communities, and because Mayfair had good assets in place, including a history of activism and leadership.

The initiative was rolled out as a community-wide planning process with two local partners—the Silicon Valley Community Foundation and the Mexican American Community Service Agency (MACS). MACS organized the planning initiative and the process of gathering information and developing a community plan. As is true of any new idea and any large community planning effort, start-up was challenging. In the end, MACS advocated that the community should form a new organization that could take on implementation of the plan. Thus was born the Mayfair Improvement Initiative. As Somos Mayfair reported in its newsletters, for ten years the Initiative was housed at the Hewlett Foundation and made direct improvements in the community, such as hiring crossing guards and adding traffic lights. The Initiative worked to improve education levels and skills of people in the community by enrolling adults in literacy, English as a second language (ESL), and GED classes. It worked to improve the school readiness of children ages zero to five. It also sought partnerships with other agencies.

The Initiative changed its name to Somos Mayfair in 2007. According to the 2007 newsletter, *Somos Mayfair* means "We Are Mayfair," an affirmation of community and a direct expression of the organization's sense of connection to its community.

Challenge Jamie Alvarado became the executive director in spring 2004. He had been with the organization since 1999 as a program director, and he was associate director prior to becoming executive director. As someone from the community, with a degree in economics and work history as an electrician, Alvarado could easily reach out and engage the community. Of course, he was not the only one, according to Alvarado. "Most of us are from this community or communities just like it. We are passionate about supporting people to overcome challenges because we have lived the same challenges."

A few short years after Alvarado became executive, the Mayfair Improvement Initiative began to separate from the Hewlett Foundation; its new name, Somos Mayfair, represented both a symbolic and real change. During the transition, the organization embraced and deepened a core belief: that people can *be* the change in their communities. This was a deep belief from the beginning of the Mayfair Improvement Initiative. The name change was thus an expression of the "heart" of the organization. The following excerpt from a 2007 organization newsletter describes the name change and its link to the more general transition.

> To many of us, when we looked forward, the name "Mayfair Improvement Initiative" would no longer accurately convey our mission or our values. The term "improvement" seemed too focused on that which was wrong about our community and the term "initiative" implied to many that our commitment was only for the short-term. Looking forward we sought a name that reflected our hopes; our belief in ourselves and our community; a name that would affirm our highest hopes for ourselves; a name focused on our greatest community asset; a name that signified our past, present and future.
>
> We chose Somos Mayfair. Somos Mayfair (We Are Mayfair) is an affirmation, an embrace, a challenge, a call and response. It is inspired in part by the civil rights struggle call from the past—"I am somebody!" The second key lesson was the importance of our stories. The stories each of us tell and live collectively form the reality of our life as a community. Thus, to tell our stories, to live out our truest stories of who we are and who we aim to be, is the first step towards creating the beloved Mayfair community of our dreams.

When Alvarado was asked about stories of organizational success, he talked about two women who were from the neighborhood.

> They have a special bond and a natural inclination to improve their lives. One is married with a family, and the other soon became divorced and a single mother. They've come to rely on each other a great deal. We got to know them through our case management system, and they were really proactive. They were interested in supporting their children to grow with pride and confidence in their Mexican heritage, so they got involved in organizing community cultural events. They wanted to show their kids that their mothers can be involved and be role models and leaders in the community. One had to overcome a stigma about being out of the house, which created problems with her husband, and the single mother kept on organizing events even though it was difficult. They do popular theater workshops, they do weeklong training institutes, and they help develop plays and workshops. While they both struggle to find steady employment, they continue to be important role models in the community and key contributors to shaping Mayfair's work. It's not a perfect ending—they didn't get a job and live happily ever after—but they are leaders in the community, and it's important and it makes a big difference in their lives.

Another example of success that Alvarado described were *promotores* (a community health educator model from Latin America). Promotores were staff who supported Mayfair families to find the resources to achieve their goals. Some of the most successful staff at Somos Mayfair were the promotores. According to Alvarado, "They exude genuine concern and caring for families, they listen and fight for their families, but they are also funny, energetic, and a joy to be around."

Alvarado indicated that, moving forward, Somos Mayfair would be more politically active in ways that reflected the immigrant community's perspective. "No one wants to leave home, but they do so because of need. The common story here is that people overcome amazing obstacles. People believe that coming here will create opportunity for themselves and their families, so they overcome incredible hardship." This belief had not been strongly held in the Mayfair Improvement Initiative. It was a new fundamental belief and assumption about the world that was part of the culture of Somos Mayfair; it came out of discussions during the transition.

It was also indicative of an immigrant worldview that observes the difference in power among various groups and will act in ways to help equalize this power.

Alvarado also noted, "One of the criticisms of the original Mayfair Improvement Initiative is that its founding framework comes out of mainstream thinking and from people who have power in society." Alvarado explained that the logical strategies and actions that spring from the mainstream power perspective "don't really make sense or have an impact" at the community level. For example, the original community planning process included primarily people who were homeowners, fully employed, or retired—the privileged members of a poor community. The strategies that came out of their participation were based on a relatively privileged point of view. So power dynamics of ownership and privilege had been in play at the origins of the Mayfair Improvement Initiative; Somos Mayfair was working to shift this perspective and embraced a view of those who had struggled to come here and might not have had economic or political influence.

Culture In this story of the beginnings of Somos Mayfair as the Mayfair Improvement Initiative and the transition away from Hewitt Foundation, we see several elements of organizational culture at play.

First was the core fundamental belief that Alvarado described as "the belief that the people in our community can be the change in our community." People with low incomes living in distressed communities can make changes, improve their lives, and increase the opportunities in their community; in fact, they may be the only ones who can. This was the single strongest operating belief (core to comprehensive community initiatives) that had led to the establishment of the Mayfair Improvement Initiative. It was a belief that was embraced and deepened during the transition and was even reflected in the explanation of the name change to Somos Mayfair.

Second was the belief that cultural heritage is important and valuable. One appropriate way to engage people from the community is to express their culture through theater and other venues. In fact, through these expressions of culture, residents can express their pride and address real issues. The new name of the organization, Somos Mayfair, was in the language of most community members and in this way highlighted the importance of the cultural history and legacy of the immigrant community in the organization. The organization assumed that the cultural traditions of immigrants are a basis for social capital—an asset that can be used to support people and their ongoing changes. This aspect of the organizational culture seemed to derive from the Mayfair community itself. The Hewlett Foundation had chosen the community for the experimental initiative because of its strong cultural legacy.

Third was the belief that peer support is powerful. Peers are the best sources of inspiration and social support during hard times. Somos Mayfair drew on peers and integrated peers through its promotores model and other aspects of its work.

Fourth was a newly emerging belief around the value and importance of expressing an immigrant worldview. At the time of our study, this belief was still being negotiated, but might be described as recognizing that people don't want to leave their homes in other countries, but do so to create economic opportunity for their families, and that those who've come here with nothing have limited economic and political power; standing up for their perspective, demonstrating their strength and their positions, is an important role for an organization claiming "Somos Mayfair" (We Are Mayfair).

Further Considerations and Reflections   Somos Mayfair succeeded in transitioning from a state of semidependence with the Hewlett Foundation. Its success in making this difficult shift was due in part to its intuitive use of organizational culture. It drew on and reinforced the core fundamental belief—of low-income people being the change in their communities. It emphasized cultural beliefs from the Latino community that it represented. These beliefs had been a part of the original organization, but were held up and broadened in the transition. By using the elements of organizational culture that already existed and finding new beliefs that were supported by the community (in other words, an immigrant worldview), Somos Mayfair successfully grew into its own strong, proud organization.

Questions

1. What would the culture of Somos Mayfair look like if, as the Hewlett Foundation scaled back funding, the organization wrote grant applications that focused on the devastating need in the community or employed a traditional social work model?

2. How might the intentional movement from a foundation-sponsored initiative to an independent organization shape the organization's culture far into the future?

EXECUTIVE DIRECTOR TRANSITION

When a nonprofit undergoes a change in executive director, it experiences a time of great challenge and great opportunity. On the challenging side, it stresses every element of the organization, including

- The board of directors, which needs to "step up" into greater leadership, take stock of the organization's direction, and determine its leadership needs—all while experiencing personal feelings of loss and grief.

- Staff, who are directly affected by the loss of one leader, by the addition of a new leader, and by job uncertainty, and who may have similar feelings of loss and grief if the executive was beloved.

- Organization systems, which may falter as a new leader learns the ropes, determines how to integrate his or her talents and knowledge into the organization, and assesses what changes need to be made.

On the opportunity side, a new leader can infuse an organization with new energy and ideas, oftentimes developing the organization in ways that may not have been previously possible.

In this section, we highlight two cases of transition from a founding executive. In one, the new executive was promoted from within; in the other, the individual was new to the organization. Their stories illustrate how understanding an organization's culture can aid the transition to stable new leadership. In our view, executive transitions, particularly those transitions from long-term or founding executives, are likely to stress beliefs and assumptions about structure, process, and leadership.

Note: Interviewing a new executive director may not yield significant information about the existing organizational culture. If the executive is very new and, like many leaders, has definitive ideas about the operations of an organization, he or she may be more focused on assessing performance and articulating his or her own vision. In examining these organizations, we gathered additional information about the organization's story and background to provide more context.

Bethel New Life: Executive Promoted from Within

Bethel New Life is a multifaceted community-based nonprofit organization serving the Garfield Park and Austin neighborhoods on the West Side of Chicago.

History Bethel New Life was formally established in 1979 by Pastor David Nelson and his sister, Mary Nelson. Pastor Nelson was the minister of Bethel Lutheran Church. The church had been an anchor in Garfield Park and Austin neighborhoods since the 1800s. In the aftermath of the riots of the 1960s with the flight of businesses and investors, Pastor Nelson and members of his congregation started a housing ministry. His sister, Mary, joined him in purchasing and rehabilitating a building. This led to the establishment of Bethel New Life as a separate nonprofit, faith-based community development corporation. Mary Nelson became its first executive director and remained in that position for twenty-four years until her retirement in 2005.

David and Mary are white, and the neighborhoods of Garfield Park and Austin are predominately African American. Mary's strong, entrepreneurial personality helped gather support and shape the organization, while David kept the organization focused on its mission and spiritual core. According to its Web site, since the 1980s, Bethel New Life has built a national reputation for faith-based approaches that focus on assets and "turning problems into possibilities through community efforts."

Challenge Steven McCullough became CEO of Bethel New Life in 2005, having previously served as its COO since 2001. He was groomed to take over the reins of Bethel New Life from Mary Nelson as she approached retirement. He came to the organization from a corporate leadership and management position, and brought with him extensive experience in creating efficient and effective operating systems. McCullough is a student of organizations, and intentionally working to understand the organizational culture of Bethel New Life had been an important part of his leadership since he arrived.

Steven described characteristics of Bethel New Life when he first arrived as entrepreneurial and high energy in doing its work, disjointed in its systems to support growth, lacking focus on the long view, and having inconsistent quality in program delivery. All the programs stood alone without a connection to an overall vision—and had historically been fragmented in this fashion. Leadership and management were centralized in Mary Nelson. McCullough noted, "As the COO, I could propose new ideas and systems, but no one would buy into changes unless Mary bought into them."

At the time of our study, as CEO, McCullough was seeing a big difference in his ability to influence change in the organization compared to when he was COO.

His aspiration was to harness the organization's entrepreneurial spirit and connection to faith, while putting practices and systems in place that strengthened the organization's capacity to serve its mission. The shift required overcoming both resistance to change and comfort with the way things had been. It also meant intentionally shifting the mind-set of staff. McCullough believed he could be successful with changing the way the organization operated once the middle layer of management bought in, but that had been challenging. Much of middle management hadn't been used to being held financially accountable, and they were reluctant to try new ideas because they hadn't received support for trying new things in the past. McCullough explained it this way: "We're changing the concentration of decision making beyond the CEO—we're working to disperse leadership and create ownership throughout the organization."

Some of the specific changes that McCullough had introduced included revamping the performance appraisal system and pay scale to reward new performance expectations. He was also leading a change around some of the organization's unwritten rules. For example, program staff did not care about program finances because the finance department was like a "black hole"— data went in but information (useful to program managers) never came out. McCullough was pushing program staff to manage program finances. He also introduced management meetings, clear agendas, and new structures to facilitate communication flow, such as meetings between divisions and programs located at different sites. At the same time that McCullough instituted these changes, he also worked to keep the organization connected to its faith and community roots. All meetings opened with something devotional that focused on mission and the desire to bring hope.

The board of directors was experiencing a lot of change as well. McCullough described this as shifting from being passive to being active, which meant taking ownership for governance rather than taking its lead from the CEO. The board also revised its bylaws to expand diversity by increasing the number of members from outside the church and reducing the number appointed through the church.

Culture   In our interview, the CEO showed a good feel for some of the main driving forces in the Bethel New Life organizational culture. He was drawing on aspects of the culture that he described in shorthand as "entrepreneurial spirit" and "faith." (We'll describe the beliefs underlying these terms later.) We suggest that the difficulty he had making some changes was evidence of where the changes were clashing with other elements of the organization's culture—described in shorthand as "strong, central leadership" and "limited systemic support for innovation."

The success of the founder's strong leadership had led the organization to assume that the right way to lead was through a central, strong figure. For twenty-four years, the organization had been successful with a single voice out front. The values of the founding leader, which could be described as optimistic and entrepreneurial, continued to pervade the organization. These founding values were also closely tied to the Lutheran Church and more generally to the role of an active faith. The beliefs from the founder and the Lutheran Church can be summarized as follows:

- Optimism and belief that working hard with God's help will yield improvements. In the founder and the organization, these values were expressed as a belief that hard work can yield success and the optimism to pursue many opportunities.
- Belief that "God calls us to be about the work of enabling the fullness of life for all" and that "God will provide," which expressed itself in an ambiguous relationship between program staff and finances.
- Belief that the right idea will succeed, so there is little need to reinforce or support program development or even consciously develop individual staff ownership.

The combination of these factors led to a general consolidation of leadership and decision making and a diminished sense of personal responsibility among program managers.

The changes McCullough was making meant that the decentralized leadership and decision making he wanted to install were bumping up against the consolidated power and leadership of the previous CEO. In addition, his emphasis on requiring program leaders to take greater responsibility for program finances met resistance from an ingrained attitude that "God calls us to do the work, and ultimately funding will be found"—that in a sense, finding funding was not the work of program staff. God would provide.

A final element of the organizational culture related to race. It is difficult to adequately describe underlying beliefs and norms around race with such brief information from a single informant. However, we believe that because of the racial tensions and devastation that prompted the founding of the organization after riots during the 1960s, there were also deep beliefs around race at the organization. At one level, there was clearly a long history of interracial engagement deeply ingrained in the organization. The initial founders (and the longtime executive) were white, but at the same time, there was a strong commitment to hiring and engaging people from the predominantly African American community. At another level, the deep racial tensions at the time of its founding undoubtedly have had other implications for the organizational culture. More information would be required to understand these.

Further Considerations and Reflections McCullough was intentionally drawing on faith roots and emphasizing certain beliefs within that faith, including optimism, hopefulness, and the call for equity and justice. His openness to the importance of organizational culture helped him take small steps and be patient with change. Moving forward, he might have been able to draw out an even deeper understanding of how the new behaviors he sought could both conflict with and build on the organizational culture.

Questions

1. What role has the church and faith had in the organization, and how are these stories relevant to its leadership today?

2. How have (or have not) program staff showed themselves to be leaders?

3. How did race play out in the founding of the organization, and how does it relate to the organization's role now? Is it possible that attempts to diversify the organization have bumped against unconscious racial issues or that beliefs around centralized leadership are intertwined with racial beliefs? Is more time necessary to discern these nuances?

Manna Food Center: Hiring from the Outside

Manna Food Center is located in Montgomery County, an affluent Maryland suburban area adjacent to Washington, DC. Manna Food Center helps feed nearly two thousand households each month. Many recipients are the working poor, some of whom work two jobs but don't have sufficient income to feed their families. With great pride, executive director Amy Ginsburg told us that Manna "fights hunger and feeds hope."

History   In 1983, Manna Food Center started when a few community leaders, including leaders of faith-based nonprofits, the religious community, businesses, and government agencies, saw a need for greater food distribution for the working poor. The story goes that this group of motivated leaders "went to a grocery store, and Manna Food Center was born." In other words, the group decided that a food center for the working poor was necessary, and they used the limited funds at their disposal to purchase food from the grocery story to begin stocking the center, which could then act as a backup to those nonprofits serving families. One of the founding entities and early "homes" for Manna was Community Ministries of Montgomery County, which has a long history as the interdenominational mechanism for congregations to address social needs in Montgomery County.

Manna Food Center was originally a fairly typical food bank, collecting food and redistributing it to nonprofits and government agencies, which then gave it directly to needy families. Within a few years, though, Manna saw a need to reach more families than they could through working with their partners and began distributing food to families as well as continuing to provide food to their nonprofit partners. In a white paper developed in 2005, Manna noted that the food delivered to partners freed up "$1 million annually, allowing scarce resources to be used by partner organizations to instead fund drug rehabilitation, life skill training, child care and shelter."

Although the client base of Manna was quite diverse, families being referred to the organization were most likely to be African American. Many clients were working, but their work history tended to be mixed and their career paths uncertain. As a part of its commitment to helping families, Manna hired staff from its client base. As Ginsburg said, this represented a commitment to "walk the talk." Manna sought to be a significant support in helping people, and what better way to help people than to employ them? Ultimately, though, Manna was about providing food; it might not address the deep roots of poverty and hunger, but it provided a safety net necessary for people to begin improving their lives.

Manna's first executive director was a government retiree who was politically well connected in the county. He was able to use his connections to "get things done," especially early on in his work at Manna. Further, his somewhat patriarchal, friendly style created a feeling of family and security at Manna. Longtime staff members at Manna talk about his willingness to listen to personal problems and stories. This openness helped connect the staff to one another and to him, creating a family atmosphere. Manna delivered over twenty million pounds of food to more than 1.7 million county residents in its first twenty years under the founding executive.

Challenge   Ginsburg succeeded the founding executive director in 2005. She said that when she heard about the position, she knew the job was for her; they just didn't know it yet. Something in the mission and the reputation of Manna as a "just do it" organization—an organization concerned with its mission of getting food out—connected with her. Ginsburg described the organization's attitude when she came in as one of "good enough"—that the organization accepted adequate performance of itself and its staff, rather than pushing for excellence. Manna was successful, but it was also unconcerned with organization systems, and at least some systems would be necessary to push for excellence. The downside she observed was that there was "a lot of inertia . . . no excitement and energy. I needed to shift the mind-set to what we could do better . . . what's best for the clients? . . . During my first week here, I spent a lot of time observing and asking how people knew things. Many of the responses were 'we just do.' No one knew how to store food and for how long, so I started paying attention to food safety and checking refrigeration; the daily reminders helped make it routine."

As the new executive director, Ginsburg wanted to make customer service and improving systems high priorities so that Manna could serve more people. "We weren't treating clients as well as we should; we said we cared, but what we did wasn't actually conveying that." Ginsburg said, "We didn't have customer service training. Sometimes staff had negative attitudes about customers." She went on to note that many staff lacked formal education; many had been clients at some point. Ginsburg strongly supported the hiring of past clients, but it also meant that there was prevalence of "the mind-set that 'rules are rules' and you can't make your own decision." Many staff had never received support for independent decision making or strategically thinking about the goal or mission and its relationship to rules. It wasn't that the rules or systems were unimportant. It was that the staff needed to be capable of making informed and caring judgments about the reason, the intent of the rules. Thus systems related to food safety would be critical because ultimately you don't want people to be sick from the food you give them, but rules on what time clients arrive or what kind of paperwork they fill out are less important.

Ginsburg worked on this by asking staff, "What would you do if this were you or your family? How would you decide about providing the emergency food or boxed lunch?" In terms of efficiency and systems, Ginsburg led by example. "I was right there loading and unloading boxes. I wasn't just talking stuff; I was modeling it." Another telling story from Ginsburg was one in which she noted that the founding executive had bailed staff out of jail, staff who may have been picked up in sweeps but hadn't done anything wrong. She continued this practice.

Ginsburg quickly encountered resistance from the administrative director. "When the previous executive director was here, the administrative director often stepped in to run things." In lieu of systems, the administrative director had been the force that helped operations. Ginsburg said, "When I came in, that went away for her. After six months, she left." Aside from the departure of the administrative director, Amy described a six-month honeymoon period. As she asked for changes that would shift the organizational operations, the general response was "Whatever you say, Amy," and staff would generally follow through at least to some degree. Some of the changes included opening earlier and on time, working on systematic storing and monitoring of food, and beginning to explore expanding programs to directly serve children.

After six months, however, Ginsburg hit a wall as staff became skeptical of her changes. Ginsburg indicated that the key to moving beyond the period of skepticism was for the staff and board to see the success of the changes she was making. For example, she ensured that Manna opened by noon every day and increased the number of families served each day. She started a new program, Smart Snacks, that in partnership with schools provided healthy food directly to children. The program not only reached an increasing number of people but brought in new corporate funding sources interested in helping hungry kids. During her first year as executive director, Ginsburg presided over a 35 percent increase in productivity without adding any additional staff. The results of her new initiatives were tangible and visible for all to see.

Culture   There were several elements in the creation story of Manna that were reflected in its organizational culture. First, the strong engagement of Community Ministries (now Interfaith Works) and other religious leaders spoke to a belief that feeding the hungry is a moral mandate. Manna wasn't created to end hunger or poverty. It was created to feed the hungry. People's basic needs must be met if they are to improve their circumstances.

Second, the founding coalition of religious, community, government, and civic leaders got Manna started by their going out and purchasing food. This approach represented a deep assumption about practicality and the idea that if we begin working we can be a positive force in the world.

Third, the founding executive used his political connections to help ensure that Manna was linked to other nonprofits and government agencies. He also created a family feeling, which reflected the belief that the agency cared for its staff and would go out of its way to support staff who were making an effort. Sometimes this belief was expressed as staff getting along and being agreeable. It might also have been expressed in the rigidity of the rules about receiving food, which helped distinguish insiders (staff) from outsiders (clients). It might also have been expressed in a patriarchal feel—an assumption that the leader will guide from above.

Fourth, a key component of Manna's culture was linked to a commitment to hiring staff from its client base. As Amy said, this was a commitment to walk the talk. The direct, practical nature of the organization was likely further reinforced by these locally hired staff and their life experiences, especially the experience of receiving food from food banks.

Further Considerations and Reflections   Ginsburg intuitively drew on these elements of culture and worked to change some artifacts or expressions of the culture and expand at least one of the beliefs—care and concern for each other— to a broader concern for the community. Building from a base of simple, direct actions (feeding the hungry) and the practical belief that by starting to act we can be a positive force for good in the world, she started new programs and expanded the numbers of people served. She also drew on some of the expressions of caring and concern for staff and on the staff's personal experience with deprivation to bring about changes in artifacts related to the way clients were treated. Intuitively, she further broadened the circle of family to include clients, paving the way for the customer service changes she wanted to accomplish. She pitched in and did the physical labor; she still bailed staff out of jail. In this way, she reinforced the caring and concern belief but began to break down the patriarchal assumption that the father stood above and over staff. With a staff drawn largely from its client base, which had reason to distrust power, her choice to model change rather than direct it was brilliant. Finally, the demonstrated success of the shifts in behavior and new programs reinforced the value of the efforts to staff and the board. Ginsburg's success appeared due to her making changes within the framework of Manna's historic culture, rather than attempting to radically change it.

Questions

1. How might dictating changes from the top and not participating in the activities of the organization rubbed against the cultural assumptions?

2. What if Ginsburg had chosen to stop hiring from the client base as a means toward greater efficiency; how would that have made change harder?

PRESSURE FROM EXTERNAL CHANGE

Particularly in the business world, organizational culture is often discussed during the postmortem of companies that were not able to adapt to a new business environment. So it isn't surprising that in a couple of the organizations we studied, it was primarily a change in the external environment—often the funding environment—that caused organizational stress and highlighted organizational culture.

In our view, the pressure of external change on nonprofits is likely to stress beliefs and assumptions about philanthropy; about how money and financial management relate to the achievement of the mission; and about the unique value of the organization—what it is, has, does, or believes that makes it different from other organizations.

DevCorps: Funding Change Creates Chaos

DevCorps is a nonprofit organization with a global reach and a domestic program. It seeks to increase economic opportunity and sustain natural resources through programs in civic engagement, agriculture, forestry, and energy. Its headquarters are in a largely rural state, but it employs over two hundred people in the United States and more than seven hundred around the world. Names and certain details have been changed to disguise the organization described in this case.

History   DevCorps was created in 1985 from the merger of three institutions—International Academic Scholarship, which provided academic scholarships to international graduate students and convened conferences; Rural Service, which provided services to developing countries to strengthen their agricultural research and development programs; and Agricultural Training Center, which was domestically focused on rural development and agriculture, with a particular interest in applying the lessons of research. Without going into detail about each of the three organizations that were merged (and thereby removing the anonymity of this story), we can note the following information about them:

1. The founders of the organizations were powerful, wealthy men from privileged backgrounds.

2. All the organizations were heavily supportive of education, scholarship, and technical, academic contributions.

3. In both of the rural-focused organizations, there was an assumption that spreading technical innovations was an important avenue to increasing productivity in agriculture.

4. There were many talented, well-known people on the boards and on staff in these organizations. On staff and acting as consultants were some of the top names in agricultural, sustainable energy, environmental, and civic engagement fields.

Although we don't have many details of the merger that resulted in the creation of DevCorps, we know that a private foundation played a significant role in supporting the merger and that there was a long and intimate relationship among the founders of the organizations and the foundation.

When our informant was asked about quintessential success stories, she chose two—one about the work of the organization in the field and one about a particularly successful staff person; both of these stories were helpful in understanding the organization. She notes that DevCorps became known for the development of a network of women who were involved in agricultural production. The network became a means of developing the leadership skills of the women and teaching them new farming practices that were also environmentally sustainable. The network became well known, and the women gained international recognition and peer support. The network also worked at the nexus of agriculture and the environment, an example of the kind of "nexus" work for which DevCorps became known.

An example of a really successful staff person was a woman who was able to cut across various units, increase communication through weekly meetings, and engage with senior management and program managers. She was an effective communicator, had a good sense of humor, and was well organized and successful. She rose quickly to a senior position in the organization.

Challenge For many years, DevCorps received sole-source contracts from the government. Shortly before the time of our study, their primary government funder moved to a new way of paying. This change had a surprising impact on the organization, because the new method of payment tends to favor a consortium, rather than a single organization, applying for contracts. In these consortiums, a large organization acts as the lead and uses subcontractors to do much of the work. Typically, this large organization is able to retain more money, making it financially healthier.

Initially, the senior management of DevCorps thought that the organization was neither large enough to be the lead in these large consortiums nor small enough to be a niche specialty subcontractor. Eventually the leadership of DevCorps decided that it was important to grow so that it could become a lead agency; at the same time, the current financial realities dictated a need for constant monitoring of the bottom line.

The decision to grow into lead-agency status and become more bottom-line oriented led to the creation of a new business department with strong and consistent internal cost recovery efforts. These new practices focused on cost cutting, leaving less funding to pay for technical expertise either on staff or from consultants. There was conflict over the new practices; some staff perceived the technical expertise as core to DevCorps and thought that the cuts make it less likely that the interventions would be successful.

Meanwhile, managers were forced to spend increased time on financial analysis and tracking and less on pursuing creative ideas and innovation. As a result, morale was down and longtime staff members were leaving, taking with them deep knowledge and the creative energy behind the organization's early success. The size of DevCorps' technical staff was consistently declining.

DevCorps leadership clearly understood the central role of innovation to the organization, as evidenced by the creation of an innovation center within the organization, where staff could write internal proposals for new projects. But managers did not have the time or energy to pursue these new proposals, and many of the ones that were being internally funded were not as grounded in technical expertise as successful projects had been in the past.

Even as the pressure was on to grow the organization financially, little time was being invested in systematically understanding the impact the work was having, or in facilitating meaningful collaboration between departments to ensure that new projects benefited from the diverse skills spread across the organization.

DevCorps staff talked about "working at the nexus of development," but doing so required integration across projects and departments, which became increasingly difficult with growth.

The organization once had a relaxed atmosphere in which its leaders often walked the halls and could converse easily with staff about any project. At the time of our study, managers said the leadership was "out of touch" and was never around their work. They felt that the leadership was making decisions separate from the reality of the work on the ground. Further, although some of the top leadership remained in place, there had been turnover, most notably in the position that led up efforts to get new business. In this case, the vice president had made a case to the board without fully engaging the president. The president had fired him effective immediately and sent out a notice to the entire company. The tension implied in that communication sent program staff running for cover. The vice president had been well liked and had been trying to fully understand the organization before making shifts.

Culture　In the story of DevCorps, its response to external pressures, and the challenges to those responses, we see manifestations of core cultural elements that were established when DevCorps was formed. Three critical values were incorporated in the organization's culture: (1) the importance of research, ideas, and innovation; (2) the value of technical expertise and competence; and (3) the belief that approaches should be grounded and locally driven.

Given these values coming out of the merger, and the conflicts our informant cited, which run in parallel with the responses to the funding changes, some of the deeply held beliefs in this organization appear to be as follows:

- Collegial attitudes, based in mutual respect for competence, proven results grown out of research, and trust, lead to the best solutions.

- Leaders should also be peers. We can solve tough environmental, energy, and agricultural issues through a scientific and technical look at what is possible—including the perspective of those who will be on the ground, using the solutions long term—and by emphasizing a willingness to be innovative and borrow ideas.

- We should be organized in ways that help highlight commonalities and lead to new ideas. Creative problem solving is extremely valuable, and anything that constrains it—such as systems or structures—is a threat.

- Integration of ideas, particularly those that come from the cross-communication among those working in different content areas, is an important source of innovation.
- Ideas that work and effort are more important than finances and systems.
- Locals must be a part of the solutions, and, with training and exposure to new technical skills, they can be effective partners in creating new opportunities in their countries.
- Forums for exchanging information—international meetings, networks, and convenings—serve an important role in building expertise and local capacity and sharing new ideas that might serve as the spark for innovation.

As DevCorps tried to grow, "going after any business" as our informant described it, the leadership might have been unconsciously trying to infuse new beliefs into the organizational culture, possibly including the importance of size in gaining respect, attracting talent, and influencing the broad global debate on development, and the idea that a better understanding of costs can yield greater efficiencies to support the work on the ground.

Depending on the ultimate success of the approach DevCorps chose, these beliefs and others that were still somewhat undefined might or might not find their way into DevCorps' deep culture. At the time of our study, DevCorps was in the midst of a culture clash between the core values of the organization and the underlying assumptions implied by the requested changes.

Further Considerations and Reflections In this story, clearly the management's choices about how to address the financial change were bumping up against some of the fundamental assumptions about innovation and the source of it that were embedded in the organizational culture. Further, the changes in structure intended to help efficiency might have been challenging beliefs about how innovation and successful projects really happen—which is through informal sharing of ideas and space to explore relationships.

DevCorps leadership could return to underlying assumptions and values with DevCorps staff to explore how their new desired financial practices might support these existing assumptions or be realigned with them, instead of moving at odds to them. Leadership could also look at how to return to inquiring, curious, and technically innovative approaches; restore effective two-way communication within the organization; increase opportunities for leadership to know staff more intimately; and better integrate strategic thinking and business development into DevCorps' mission-driven work. Another area of inquiry would be into how the organization creates and sustains trust and technical capacity.

Building trust and a high level of technical capacity had been important to DevCorps' international success, but new processes might be undermining those values inside the organization. If the organization were to continue to ignore the parts of its culture that contributed to its early success, it may lose key personnel and the qualities that made it a great place to work and accomplish an important mission. As a result, the organization may enter a phase of slow decline. In essence, DevCorps leadership could benefit from looking closely at the existing underlying assumptions that have shaped the organization to date and thinking about ways to draw on these assumptions in making the argument for change.

A more radical shift would be for the leadership to revisit the decision to attempt to become a lead agency, seeking a different funding model to keep its successes going. It is possible that the culture necessary to succeed as a lead agency is incompatible with the culture necessary to succeed as an innovative and technical agency.

Questions

1. What specific behavior might the organization focus on shifting?

2. How could DevCorps leaders draw on a particular aspect of its culture to help support that change?

LEDC: Meeting the Needs of a Changing Immigrant Community

Latino Economic Development Corporation (LEDC) in Washington, DC, was created in 1991. LEDC's mission is to improve the wealth-building capacity of low- and moderate-income Latinos and other underserved communities in the Washington area.

History Through the 1980s, there was a growing community of Central American (primarily El Salvadoran and Nicaraguan) refugees in the District of Columbia. Many of these refugees had lost everything, including family members. Ward 1, where Mt. Pleasant is located, had become a Latino enclave; this immigrant community had little municipal power or political access.

When the head of a "Latino underground bank" (an informal bank for the community) took off with the assets and a DC police officer shot an intoxicated El Salvadoran, the rage resulted in a weeklong riot. Then a federal investigation also found routine discriminatory practices in local government, and the mayor was instructed to create the Latino Civil Rights Task Force. LEDC was an outgrowth of the task force's work.

According to Manny Hidalgo, the executive director at the time of our study, LEDC was established on the principle that "the community would not be stable until there is a strong economy where people in the community are owners of homes and businesses; that unless you have an owning class, the residents will not see the value of maintaining the community. Ultimately its aim is to transcend economics and help new Latino residents become a political power. LEDC started with the premise that the Latino community was staying in DC and had a right to be part of the economic and the political power structure."

Challenge The environment in which LEDC operated at the time of this case study (2007) had completely changed since its founding in 1991. Ward 1, where LEDC is located, and adjacent Ward 4 were experiencing significant gentrification, making it difficult for the organization's Latino clients to become homeowners. Many were moving to other, more affordable areas, but returned to the community to maintain the businesses they had created. Further, other parts of DC (Wards 7 and 8) were interested in attracting Latino residents to help diversify their communities. As a result of these external changes, LEDC shifted its strategies. It was now working to help as many Latinos as possible become homeowners and business owners, rather than to improve a particular community in DC. LEDC continued to work to integrate communities that had significant Latino populations into the economic mainstream.

LEDC had undergone a succession of executive directors over the past several years. It had been challenged to find candidates from the Latino community who had the right mix of leadership, political, and management skills required for effectiveness in dealing with the political aspects of the organization's work. It had had five permanent executive directors, including the current director, Manny Hidalgo, who had been in the role for just over two years when we interviewed him.

Hidalgo is the child of Cuban refugees and a graduate of a prestigious college, with extensive professional experience in team building and leadership development. He described himself as "the product of a welcoming country that gave his family many opportunities through the Cuban enclave in Miami." His experience in 1961 differed greatly from the experience of Central American refugees in 1991, and this was not lost on him in working at LEDC. He wanted to "pay forward" the opportunity he had been given.

Hidalgo described the organization's most significant accomplishments as "helping people recognize their power—acknowledging it, helping them see they can use it, helping them use it, and recognizing their success in using it."

In the context of executive transition and significant changes in its operating environment, LEDC was experiencing three particular organizational pressures:

1. It was becoming a regional organization with new growth to manage. It had recently opened a second office in Maryland.

2. Along with this growth came the need to retain and reward good staff by giving them interesting work and competitive compensation.

3. The breadth of the work that LEDC was taking on was large—it worked with individuals and communities and continued to advocate for public policies that preserve small, independent businesses and diverse homeowners. Hidalgo believed that as an economic development organization, LEDC should be able to be a leader in creating the triple bottom line of achieving social change, protecting the environment, and earning revenue.

To manage these pressures, Hidalgo was working to decentralize decision making as much as possible and to create collective leadership and shared responsibility at all levels of the organization. (In this way, the LEDC experience is similar to the Bethel New Life leadership transition story.) Not surprisingly given the complex and interrelated beliefs incorporated within LEDC, the notion of dispersed leadership and responsibility turned out to be a messy one to execute as the management team took it on but had not been able to push it further into the organization. The question of what decentralized leadership meant for this organization had not yet been clearly articulated.

Culture In the tension that was created by Hidalgo's attempts to change assumptions about leadership and decision making and by the external pressures of a changing community environment, we see evidence of some of the core cultural elements of LEDC:

- The Latino community in DC deserves and needs a political power base.

- An activist orientation that uses an adversarial-conflict model for creating political pressure is the appropriate means of seeking political power.

- Political power alone does not give people sufficient stake in the care and improvement of a community. Economic opportunity and ownership are important, especially for Central American refugees who arrive with no assets and, in many cases, few employable skills. (These beliefs were in some tension: one created instability in the community through political tactics, and the other sought stability through ownership. However, this tension had been held within LEDC since its founding.)

- In order to be authentic in its political leadership, LEDC must be led by someone of the Latino community and preferably someone with direct experience with Central American refugee families.

The organizational culture was also influenced by beliefs and values from Latino cultures, including a tendency toward strong, centralized, hierarchical, male leadership and decision making. There was a tendency for Latino staff to "wait for the leader to speak." This was further exacerbated in the case of LEDC because staff members who were Central American in origin tended not to be vocal, whereas Hidalgo, who is of Cuban origin, was quite a bit more outspoken. So LEDC staff and constituents tended to expect a strong central leader who would give clear direction and who would not need them to offer much input into decision making.

Finally, intertwined in LEDC's organizational culture was the complexity and diversity of Latinos' experiences here in the United States. Latino immigrants are from many different countries in Central and South America and from Cuba. LEDC assumed a certain commonality of experience among these different immigrant groups. At the same time, even in the early days of the task force, there were differences among different Latino groups. This tension was embedded within LEDC.

Further Considerations and Reflections   LEDC was born out of an environment of intense conflicts (riots) in a specific geographic and ethnic community.

This is one key to understanding the embedded assumptions that shaped its culture. Further, its underlying Latino community culture tended to support strong, hierarchical leadership. However, LEDC had grown into a regional organization that required the relaxation of both central authority and geographic focus. Hidalgo hoped to decentralize decision making, which would appear to be at odds with the organization's expectation of concentrated authority. Given the culture, he might need to seek some overarching organizational cultural story (one that is common across many Latino cultures) that highlighted the importance of dispersed leadership, and to draw on this story to help him make those changes.

In addition, LEDC was born as a grassroots, refugee-serving organization. Hidalgo, though a child of refugees, did not directly share the experience. Further, he brought an academic training and background that differed dramatically from the grassroots background of the organization. A deeper understanding of the organization's culture would enable Hidalgo to see ways in which it would support him because of his background, and ways in which it might oppose him. This would help him determine means of assisting staff in working through their resistance to the changes he intended to make.

Although this case did not explore the history of LEDC's five executive directors in its relatively short history, one has to question both the influence of the culture on such rapid turnover and the impact of rapid turnover on the culture.

Questions

1. How might revisiting LEDC's creation story and the assumptions about building an ownership class that is politically powerful help support Hidalgo's desired changes?

2. What other kinds of organization stories might be helpful to hear from staff?

REFLECTIONS: USING STORIES TO ILLUMINATE NONPROFIT ORGANIZATIONAL CULTURE

We hope the stories in this chapter begin to illustrate how unearthing buried aspects of organizational culture can aid nonprofits and their leaders. In each example, the stories told by our informants helped us uncover deeply held assumptions that were rising to the surface and bumping up against contemporary stressors. The process of describing these deeply held beliefs enabled us to better understand the challenges facing the leader and the organization. This, in turn, helped us think more carefully about strategies the leader could consider for accomplishing the sought-after change, or ponder whether the change itself should be reconsidered.

As a closing reflection, we'd like to highlight several ideas that crystallized for us in developing these stories.

Discovering Themes

As we wrote these stories, we looked for themes—phrases and images that were common across multiple stories. We used intuition, our broad base of experience in nonprofit capacity building and with typical nonprofit challenges, and our knowledge of organizational culture. Specifically, we combined our knowledge of the category of challenge (life cycle change, executive transition, external pressure) with the stories told by the informants. As we did so, we paid special attention to creation and survival stories. This framework helped us see the challenge facing the organization from a broader perspective and helped us look for assumptions in the stories people told.

For example, in the Somos Mayfair story, we heard similar language of community residents changing their communities to improve their own lives. This theme was reflected in the creation of the Mayfair Improvement Initiative and became very clear in the transition to Somos Mayfair. In the story of Arctusis, we saw that strong, willful leadership had led to success during its early years, but now made change very difficult.

Or consider Bethel New Life, which faced a transition from the founding executive to a new leader. Here, we saw that the organization's creation had included strong connections to the church's hierarchical structure, a belief in the value of faith (the sense that "God will provide"), and an assumption that "if we work hard enough, we'll succeed." These same elements, carried into the organization's present-day situation, had influenced staff to shy away from dispersed leadership and avoid attempts to change practices. At the same time, these elements helped staff retain a strong sense of the role faith played in their work. Stated so simply, one can see that the resistance to change and the *solution* to that resistance were both available in Bethel New Life's culture.

Identifying Ways Cultural Elements Helped and Hindered

After we had identified themes—underlying assumptions that form the scaffolding of culture—we considered ways that the culture was either helping or hindering the organization in its attempts to address its current challenge. These stories continued to convince us that leaders are better equipped to lead an organization through change and stress when they understand its culture, even though most of these leaders were doing this intuitively (as opposed to systematically). For example, Somos Mayfair recognized that it had a historical belief in the wisdom of its constituent community and their cultural assets, such as community theater. These elements could continue to feed the growth and grounding of the organization. In the case of Bethel New Life, the new executive director was positioned to explore how cultural assumptions around leadership resulted in staff's being reticent about taking on dispersed leadership. He had an opportunity to capitalize on another cultural element—the entrepreneurial, can-do spirit—as a way to move the organization closer to the form of dispersed leadership that it now needed.

Unearthing Nonprofit Culture

One thread across many of the organizations was that several of the core beliefs and assumptions of the culture were probably unique to nonprofits. Bethel New Life's connection to faith was typical of faith-based nonprofit organizations. Some of those deep assumptions were that working hard with God's help will yield improvements, God calls us to be about the work of enabling the fullness of life for all, and God will provide. All of these beliefs were central to Bethel New Life culture. For Manna, a central belief was that feeding the hungry is a moral imperative. For Somos Mayfair and LEDC, some core beliefs were reflective of their activist beliefs. For Somos Mayfair, this belief centered around the importance of the immigrant worldview and standing up for immigrants. For LEDC, there were twin activist beliefs: the Latino community in DC deserves and needs a political power base, and an adversarial-conflict model for creating political pressure is the appropriate means of seeking political power.

If we were working with the organizations in this chapter on a continuous basis, we might take this analysis another step by looking at the nonprofit theories we discussed in Chapter One, assigning each organization to a theory or two and then looking explicitly for assumptions about issues predicted by the theory. For example, DevCorps is well explained by innovation theory—that nonprofits arise from the public's need for new services and products and the government's inability to act on this need until there is some certainty around the approach. A subset of innovation theory is the idea that nonprofits arise to provide greater flexibility in the provision of public services. Innovation theory suggests that the nonprofit would have resolved specific and important beliefs around research, trying new ideas, and flexibility, and that the nonprofit is likely to have close and somewhat contradictory conversations about their relationship with government. Even with the limited information that we have about DevCorps, we can see that innovation theory has suggested some important issues for the organization to examine.

As another example, civic diversity theory, which claims that nonprofits arise as a means and mechanism for allowing greater, more diverse participation in public life, sheds light on Arctusis, Somos Mayfair, and LEDC. Civic diversity theory suggests that there will be strong beliefs about participation in public debate and around diversity and tolerance. Again we can already see that these are important parts of the cultural territory for these organizations.

Relating Organizational Stressors to Cultural Analysis

Upon reflection, we wonder if the kind of challenge or stress an organization is undergoing can help us be more targeted in our exploration of organizational culture. The challenge or stressor is likely to create common and predictable management problems, and the responses to these management issues may or may not conflict with elements of the organization's culture. For example, Bethel New Life's executive transition created predictable management challenges around leadership, and its transition from a founding executive (a life cycle change) raised management issues around structure. The extent to which these came into conflict with the cultural elements at Bethel New Life depended on the specific assumptions of the culture and the response of management. In Bethel's case, the transition confronted assumptions around strong central leadership and structure. The new executive wanted more dispersed leadership and accountability, as well as changes in financial systems. However, the same assumptions about leadership (strong leader knows best) were also helping the new executive have some success in addressing the changes in system behaviors.

The external pressures to change can be incredibly varied and can create a plethora of management issues. However, there is often a strategy element to these issues, as strategy inevitably deals with matching of current resources to environmental circumstances. Let's take DevCorps as an example. In this case, the external pressure from funder changes led to a decision to change strategy and become a lead agency. The specifics of management's response conflicted with several deep organizational assumptions about the role of technical expertise and the way that innovation is created, but we can imagine ways that leadership's response would have been less likely to conflict with the culture. For example, if management had been more aware of the culture, it might have sought to make the changes in ways that encouraged participative buy-in from the professional staff rather than using top-down, command-and-control approaches. It might have encouraged staff to innovate new responses to the external threat, thereby capitalizing on the culture's strong thread of innovation and emphasis on peer relationships.

Through these interviews, we learned a great deal about uncovering and describing an organization's culture. We confirmed the importance of stories and narratives, we practiced a process of identifying themes and articulating beliefs, we used our analysis to make suggestions to current leaders, and we began to explore how we could continue the analysis using nonprofit theories. In the next chapter, we offer the fruit of these lessons and other elements of our learning: a process for identifying and describing a nonprofit's culture.

Revealing Organizational Culture

O rganizational culture begins to emerge the moment the idea of an organization is formed. It resides in the deepest unconscious aspects of all organizations. It is an intangible concept that becomes tangible through the way that people in organizations come to understand it and act it out in their beliefs, relationships, and behavior. Organizational culture touches every person in every organization, influencing the way they relate to one another and to other organizations, and flavoring every aspect of the way the organization approaches its work, conducts its programs, and records and celebrates its successes.

But organizational culture does not easily yield its secrets. Truly understanding a culture requires a commitment to intentional and time-consuming exploration.

In the previous chapter, we explored organizational culture using real organizations. We learned how understanding these cultural elements can help organization leaders who are facing significant challenges. As consultants and authors, we also learned we had the makings of a more comprehensive process than currently exists for bringing organizational culture to the surface—one that would help you assess and describe your organization's culture and how that culture may help or hinder plans you have for your organization.

In this chapter, we share our process through the example of a nonprofit organization with which each of us is familiar. We found that by illustrating each step of the process in a way that demonstrates how to use intuition and interpretation, we could bring greater clarity to our approach. Please note that the name of the example organization, along with some of its characteristics, has been changed to protect its identity. We're calling this organization the Human Rights Institute (HRI). We call our tool *ROC,* for *Revealing Organizational Culture.*

THE RELATIONSHIP BETWEEN ROC AND OTHER CULTURE TOOLS

Our tool, ROC, draws heavily on the work of Edgar Schein. We've chosen to use Schein's ideas as a frame for several reasons. First and most important, we concur with Schein about the depth and complexity of organizational culture and with his conclusion that the only way to truly understand an organization's culture is from its own perspective and its own experiences. We prefer this approach to models that start with typologies or categories, apply those categories to the organization, and move inward. As Schein argues, "typologies can be useful if we are trying to compare many organizations but can be quite useless if we are trying to understand one particular organization" (2004, p. 190). Schein's understanding of organizational culture and how to approach it is based on fundamental tenets of anthropology, and we think that this approach is most likely to yield accurate insights.

Second, we think Schein's process is reflective of an appreciative inquiry approach that will feel comfortable and somewhat familiar to many nonprofit leaders, managers, and capacity builders. Further, the process of working with a group within an organization to sift through organizational experience and identify key elements of culture, as Schein does, is a participatory process that builds commitment to the results and implications. Finally, Schein also offers explicit suggestions for what to do with the information about organizational culture that has been gathered. We think that this is an important benefit of his approach.

We've added to Schein's process, however. Our emphasis on the importance of stories and narratives is certainly consistent with Schein, but he does not highlight them as we do. We believe you can obtain a more rounded, holistic view of an organization's culture by intentionally gathering certain types of information about the organization and sharing specific types of stories. We have also added a few analytical tools that may help organizations connect to different aspects of the culture. Finally, we suggest that organizations create a description of the core elements of organizational culture to use as a point of reference in other management discussions moving forward.

LEARNING THROUGH STORIES

We identify three particular kinds of stories that are critical sources of information about organizational culture: *the creation story, survival stories,* and *heroic or successful staff stories.* Through our research, we found that these types of stories are usually filled with images, values, and assumptions, and with characters who acted on these values and assumptions. We found analyzing these stories to be the most powerful way to surface the "hidden truths" about organizational culture.

Three particular kinds of stories are critical sources of information about organizational culture: the creation story, survival stories, and heroic or successful staff stories.

The *creation story* is a "thick" description of who formed the organization and why. (*Thick* is anthropologists' jargon for "richly described and full of meaning.") The creation story should include information about why the organization was created, what it was intended to accomplish, who founded it, how they founded it, and information about the broader environment at the time of the creation. In this story is evidence of the most important solutions to problems and of behaviors that dealt with uncertainties; these solutions became the core beliefs and assumptions at the heart of the organization's culture. (See "Creation Story" in the section phase 2, step 3 for suggested questions to ask in order to reveal the creation story.)

A good illustration of how an organization's creation story continues to shape its culture many years later is the following example about a management support organization in the Midwest. The organization was founded in the late 1960s, when, as Bob Dylan sung in what became a generation's anthem, "The times they are a changin'." An unpopular war overseas, growing racial militancy, and increasing use of drugs deemed illegal by the "powers that be" all contributed to a combustible mix that infused many of the organizations created at that time with a belief that conflict and confrontation with those representing the "establishment" were appropriate and necessary. The organization was originally founded as a resource to train VISTA volunteers and place them in community action projects. Its culture incorporated the anti-establishment spirit of the time. Although its mission evolved to one that offered a broader array of services to community agencies, the organization's core beliefs about power institutions and its role in confronting these institutions did not shift.

Nearly thirty years after its founding, the organization was distributing material describing capitalism as the "enemy" while soliciting support from corporations and wealthy individuals. Although some stakeholders recognized the need to change the culture, these efforts were met with resistance by leadership. As one of the organization's leaders said at the time, "We need to be faithful to those who came before us." This comment certainly speaks to the difficulty, if not the impossibility, of changing the fundamental nature of organizational culture without a clear understanding of how the organization's creation story continues to shape its beliefs for those who see themselves as "keepers" of the organizational culture.

Survival stories are also thick narratives, but this type focuses on extreme life-threatening challenges that an organization has successfully faced. Survival stories are meant to be about those times when people within the organization really thought it might close or might not survive in its current form. These stories are not supposed to be rudimentary sketches of how the organization succeeded in getting a new grant or in integrating a new program (the kind of normal upgrades and changes in processes that every organization must undergo). When you have heard a survival story, you should be able to articulate what the threat to the organization was, why it was so serious, and what the organization did to successfully navigate this threat. Because survival stories are about "life and death," the story should endure; there should be indications that this is a lasting story. (See "Survival Story" in the section phase 2, step 3 for suggested questions to ask to reveal a survival story.)

Here is an example of a true survival story. When the founding executive director of twenty-five years died of a massive coronary in his office at the emergency shelter for runaway and homeless youth, the organization went into a downward spiral. Staff and board felt the tragic loss of a charismatic and beloved leader and friend. The organization had no management systems in place to help it operate without the knowledge of the founder. The organization's offices and the shelter were in serious disrepair, with state inspections looming. There was no plan or resources to clean things up adequately, and the state had committed funds to build a new shelter some sixty miles away in another part of the county.

The board members were gravely concerned—they didn't know how to find the right person to stabilize the situation or support existing staff.

How did the organization deal with this crisis? First, the board (in particular the board chair) stepped forward and began asking questions. Once the board chair understood how desperate things where, he worked over the course of several meetings with other board members and top staff to convince others that they had to share the full depth of the problem with a major stakeholder and funder. Although many were worried that this would send a disastrous message to some of their few remaining supporters, they ultimately agreed. Board leaders went to the United Way, laid their cards on the table, and asked for help. The process of negotiation and the ultimate act of faith in going to a closely held outside group say a great deal about the organization's core beliefs around their role in the community and the right way to get things done. Because the leaders asked, United Way did in fact help with interim leadership that put the organization on a new path.

Finally, we look at stories of the really successful staff person; we call this the story of the "hero or heroine" because often the stories around this individual have magical or mythical qualities. In these stories, the person becomes larger than life. Remember that your goal is to capture the story that is told and retold about this staff person, not necessarily just the facts. In this case you are looking for stories that are told about a super-successful staff person. Sometimes these stories will be told as "the way things used to be," and they often represent a norm about the way the organization operates (or operated). These stories can be tricky to find. They don't have to be about something that the organization is particularly proud of or that the organization would publicize to others; these are often internal stories.

For example, there was a particularly successful national training organization that had a reputation for creating transformative training for leaders. The hero story in this organization was about the first trainer, and the story went something like this: "When he was doing trainings, there wasn't much planning about the particulars of the session. You know, 'We'll design no training before its time.' This meant 'We'll design the training the night before.' But he'd get in there, and it was just amazing; he'd connect with everyone. He really knew how to draw on the group. By the end, people were thrilled; they were amazed and deeply engaged. Then we'd spend half the night drinking beers and talking about the implications and the field as a whole with everyone." This story

BEFORE YOU BEGIN

As you start out on your journey to discover your organization's culture, you need to consider a few essential points that will help ensure success.

Consider Using a Skilled Facilitator

It is difficult to look objectively at your own organization. When you're in the middle of the action, it is all but impossible to see the big picture. This is why multiple people must be involved in the process and why the organization's leader(s) must follow the metaphorical advice of Heifetz and Linsky in their book *Leadership on the Line* to go "up to the balcony and look down on the dance floor. . . . the only way you can gain both a clearer view of reality and some perspective is by distancing yourself from the fray" (2002, p. 53). Many organizations have experienced the benefit of retaining a consultant not connected with the organization to facilitate their strategic planning. This is a worthy consideration for getting help to discover your organizational culture.

Listen for What's Hard to Hear

Remain open to learning the truth about your organization: success ultimately comes from struggling with things that may be difficult to hear. Max De Pree, author of several notable books on leadership, stated it this way in a conversation with the late Peter Drucker: "The first duty of a leader is to define reality. Every organization, in order to be healthy, to have a renewal process, to survive, has to be in touch with reality" (Drucker, 2006, p. 40). We believe that the process of discovering and understanding organizational culture provides a unique opportunity for organization leaders and staff to be honest about what your organization *is,* not what you wish it were or hope it might be. It might be helpful to know that *every* organization's culture has elements that help move it forward and aspects that create drag. Culture is by its nature a conservative, stabilizing force—remember that humans create culture to deal with uncertainty. Don't cover up or deny the aspects of your organization's culture that are creating a drag on staff morale, funding, programming, and so on.

Trust Your Instincts

Surfacing organizational culture is "left-brain work" because it requires you to tap your intuition and move iteratively between inductive and deductive reasoning. When you do this work, you'll be moving from small concepts to big ideas and from big ideas to small concepts. This work is an art and a science. At some points, you'll collect specific factual information; at others, you'll interpret meaning using intuition. Intuition is a "knowing" or sensing; in this process you'll explore your organization through a new lens that will help you know some of the deeper parts of your organizational culture.

doesn't portray some perfect ideal of how training is supposed to be created, nor is it entirely true (in reality, there *was* some preplanning). However, it is the story that is told. (See "Hero or Heroine Story" in the section phase 2, step 3 for suggested questions to ask to find hero and heroine stories.)

REVEALING ORGANIZATIONAL CULTURE (ROC): A PROCESS FOR INTERNAL AND EXTERNAL CONSULTANTS

Our process for surfacing the hidden truths about organizational culture is divided into four phases, described briefly in the list that follows. We focus on explaining how to gather and analyze information, show how to describe the hidden truths of your organization's culture, and explore ways of using this information to help achieve particular objectives.

Phase 1: Prepare. In this phase, you gain a basic understanding of the organization and its context and identify management's interests in organizational culture.

Phase 2: Gather Culture Stories and Interpret Meaning. In this phase, you define what the group working to describe the organizational culture wants to achieve (its objective), gather information in the form of stories and other discussions about the organization's behavior, and then develop a short description of (at least part of) the organization's culture.

Phase 3: Assess Implications for the Objective and Your Plan. In this phase, you consider how your organization's culture (now "revealed" by your organizational culture description) can help or hinder the organization in addressing the stated objective; then you create a plan for building on the existing culture, adding new elements to the culture, or possibly shifting existing elements.

Phase 4: Define Intentional Action and Implementation Plan. In this phase, you focus on how change happens and emphasize the support and intention needed to implement your plans.

Because this is a comprehensive process and meant to be useful to anyone, there may be pieces of information that we refer to that are less important to your particular situation. As we move through the process, we note those practices that could provide additional clarity but may not be necessary. We also offer lots of tips about facilitating meetings.

Phase 1: Prepare

In the preparation phase, you collect basic information about the organization and its context (its unique circumstances or situation). This data collection or compilation should be conducted with broad strokes and takes only a couple of hours; the sources are published documents, Web sites, and a single forty-five minute interview with top management. The idea is simply to give you enough background to draw on later in your discussions. You should avoid acquiring so much information that you begin to draw conclusions. (We emphasize the broad nature of this data collection because many organization development consultants will be inclined to go deeper at this early stage.)

If you work at the organization, this phase may entail simply taking the time to summarize what you already know; if you're a consultant assisting the organization, this is information you might gather in your first few contacts with the client. Either way, gather the facts about the organization and compile them in a brief summary. If you visit the organization's offices, you may also want to be aware of the look and feel of the office. *Everything you gather in this phase will be relevant in phase 2.* The following sections list questions to consider during this phase.

Organization Identity   Collect basic information about the identity of the organization.

- What is the mission statement?
- What is the vision statement?

- What are the stated core operating values?

- What other similar organizations are in its networks and "peer circle"? (This may help you begin to get a sense of the approach the organization takes; it is not critical information.)

- What are the dominant funding sources or strategies (for example, government contracts or membership)?

Organization Size and Structure   Collect preliminary factual information about the organization.

- How big and distributed is the organization (how many staff members, locations)?

- What are its major programs?

Top Management Perspective   Interview top management to gather additional background that frames questions for the group discussion in phase 2. The interview requires approximately forty-five minutes; you should focus particularly on what top management wants to achieve from examining organizational culture and the basic creation story.

Keeping those foci in mind, the following are questions to help guide the interview.

1. Briefly ask them to tell you about how the organization was formed and a little about its founders.

2. Ask *briefly* about the current situation:

   - What is the organization's major challenge?

   - What are a few of its major accomplishments and strengths?

   - Are a significant number of staff or board members relatively new to the organization?

   - Is there a lot of turnover? (You may need to take this into account as you form your group for phase 2.)

3. What is the objective for the work you'll be doing with regard to organizational culture? In other words, from management's perspective, what do they want to see achieved through the inquiry into organizational culture? Most top leaders will be able to identify a specific change or result. You

may begin the questions about the objective for the work by asking some or all of the following:

- What is driving the interest in organizational culture?

- Why is the organization thinking about its culture? (You may draw on current challenges or issues that you just talked about.)

- Who within the organization is driving this effort?

- Is there something that is not working very well for the organization that you want this effort to "fix"?

- What are the signs of dissatisfaction? What are people asking for? How are staff or other stakeholders showing their displeasure?

Compile a brief written summary of all the information collected in phase 1. You will want to use the information as a backdrop for the group discussion in phase 2. Exhibit 3.1 summarizes the data gathered at the Human Rights Institute during phase 1.

Phase 2: Gather Culture Stories and Interpret Meaning

Phase 2 is the heart of the process for surfacing your organizational culture. Remember, an organization's culture is built from its specific circumstances, and it is the property of the group. Therefore, organizational culture will be easiest to unearth in a group situation. The synergy of individuals thinking and talking together will result in revelations and discoveries that simply cannot be produced by speaking with people individually. This is especially important when so much of what is to be learned lies invisible beneath the surface. It is important that the group that is formed feel able to share stories about the organization. A couple of ways to support the necessary trust are to draw group members from a cross section of the organization but not from different hierarchical levels and to secure the strong support of the organization's leadership and their acknowledgment that challenging stories might be told.

The group of people that is gathered for this phase is somewhat dependent on the size of the organization and the objective of the work. If it is a small organization, you will likely want to have everyone involved. If it is larger, you'll want a good cross section of the organization. You'll also want most people (although not all) to have been with the organization for a year or more so that they are likely to have heard the stories and can describe the things you ask about.

Exhibit 3.1
HRI Phase 1—Prepare

Preparation Category	Data Collection Questions	Responses
Organization Identity	What is the mission statement?	Protect the human rights of political prisoners and victims of torture.
	What is the vision statement?	A world where every human being is protected against life-threatening injustice.
	What are the stated core operating values?	• Human life is sacred. • Treat all people with dignity and respect. • Uphold safety, freedom, and human rights. • Commit to continual learning.
	What field or subsector of the nonprofit sector does the organization call home?	Human rights advocacy.
	What other similar organizations are in its networks and "peer circle"?	Not critical for this case.
	What is the dominant funding source or strategy?	Church donations and government grants.
Organization Size and Structure	Staff size	Seventy-five
	Structure	Hierarchical
	Annual budget	$25 million
	Major programs	• Policy advocacy • Legal services
	Tenure of board and management-level staff	Lengthy board member tenure; the average tenure for senior staff is ten to twenty years.

(continued)

Exhibit 3.1 *(continued)*

Preparation Category	Data Collection Questions	Responses
Top Management Perspective	Creation story (brief)	The organization formed as an alliance of churches seeking to protect the rights of people persecuted and tortured for their political beliefs in a country with a totalitarian regime.
	Major issues (if any) facing the organization	• The organization is having difficulty raising sufficient funds to support quality international programs. • A recent staff survey shows that employees do not believe HRI's leadership takes their needs and opinions into account when making decisions. • There is high turnover among middle managers and program staff.
	What are a few of its major accomplishments?	• National conference attracted four hundred participants. • Two regional conferences attracted one hundred participants each. • Pro bono legal counsel was delivered to twenty-five hundred individuals.
	What is driving the interest in organizational culture?	Being heavily dependent on government funding has constrained the organization for many years in terms of doing the most creative work it can to advance its mission. Although there have been ongoing conversations about reducing this dependency, no significant progress has been made to do so. In addition, there is great dissatisfaction among

	staff responsible for directing and delivering programs and services with regard to the leadership and management style in the organization.
What are the signs of dissatisfaction?	There is a revolving door in middle management positions, as well as a lack of confidence and trust in senior management, expressed in a recent anonymous survey of staff.
Who within the organization is driving the effort?	Senior management.
How is the organization planning to use the knowledge about its organizational culture? What is likely to be different as a result?	Senior management believes that significant work needs to be done to change how the organization raises money, and it needs strong and energized middle management to be enthusiastic participants. The leaders also desire to reduce staff dissatisfaction and turnover.

(*Note:* If there is significant turnover in the organization, this last suggestion may be difficult to follow; you may even need to draw on past board or staff members who left relatively amicably.) You may also consider the objective of the work and include a mix of the people who are most likely to be engaged in work on that objective.

We suggest that prior to the meeting, you help participants prepare by sharing a meeting agenda, the summary of organization information you collected in phase 1 (make sure there is nothing from the top management interview they don't want broadly shared), and a definition of organizational culture. (You may also want to prepare a handout defining organizational culture to provide at the meeting.)

Following is a sample agenda for this group discussion:

Step 1: Review and discuss the definition of organizational culture
(15 minutes)

Step 2: Define the objective for examining organizational culture (20 minutes)

Step 3: Share stories and create a mind map (2.5 hours)

Step 4: Analyze the stories and reveal hidden truths in the culture (1 hour)

Facilitation Tips

- To put yourself in the right frame of mind for open, nonjudgmental listening, you might imagine yourself as a reporter who will be writing an in-depth story on the meeting. Just like a reporter, you have done a little background research (phase 1) so that you can ask good questions. You need to be able to report on everything, from what it felt like to be there to what people actually said. You will not know until the meeting has concluded what the lead for the story will be or even what quotes or comments will be relevant. Consequently, you will want to take particularly good notes. You may even record the session or have someone take notes with you. You should use all your senses; employ the questions and tools in the process to help capture information, but do not let them limit what you record. Ask yourself, would someone else who was not in attendance be able by reading your notes to get a clear, correct picture of what you observed?

- Listen closely and openly without judgment to the stories that people tell about the organization; ask for as much description as people can give.

- Record the stories that people share along with the group's overall reaction to the stories or statements. For example, if one person tells a story about heroic staff and the rest of the room is quiet or noncommittal afterwards, you may need to look further for a story that truly resonates with the group. In looking for more information, don't tell people they are wrong; instead say, "Can you tell me more?" or "Great. Does someone have another example?"

Phase 2, Step 1: Review and Discuss the Definition of Organizational Culture You'll want to spend a few minutes making sure that everyone understands the definition of organizational culture. Ask participants to put the definition into their own words. (See the section Defining Organizational Culture in Chapter One.)

Phase 2, Step 2: Define the Objective for Examining Organizational Culture During your interview with top management, you should have identified a preliminary objective they want to address by understanding the organization's culture. Share this with the group. Ask if there are other compelling issues facing the organization today—these can be internal or external—and what specifically the participants would like to see be different because of this examination of culture. Ideally these will be similar to what the top management identified. If you don't have agreement, you will need to create a process for getting everyone on the same page in terms of the objective of this organizational culture inquiry.

In defining the objective for the work, remember to be as specific as you can. Don't let the group simply use words like "improved teamwork" or "better communication" or "more efficient." They must be specific about what they mean and what they want to see in the organization—that is, they must say what improved teamwork, communications, or efficiency will look like. You can come back to this objective throughout the meeting and refine it if you need to.

Exhibit 3.2
HRI Phase 2, Step 2—Description of the Objective

The following is an example of a preliminary objective for the Human Rights Institute: Middle management needs to be involved in new fundraising strategies, but first middle management turnover must be reduced. Middle managers have said that better communication with senior management would be likely to reduce turnover. Communication should be characterized as follows: open (where both sides are able to raise issues and have discussion), regular (at least once a week), and mutually respectful (no personalization of issues; serious consideration of others' perspectives and ideas); consistent messages should be created by the group as a whole.

Phase 2, Step 3: Share Stories and Create a Mind Map   In this part of the meeting, you will be gathering stories about the organization and other information to create a mind map of aspects of your organization's culture. A mind map is a visual, nonlinear technique for recording information (Buzan and Buzan, 1996). It is organized around a central concept with elements categorized as branches that radiate around the central idea. Mind maps are used to generate, visualize, and structure ideas and to aid in problem solving. They can contain descriptive words, or pictures if participants would rather draw concepts. We suggest using a mind map because it makes visible the elements of culture by placing diverse key concepts from stories next to one another. Figure 3.1 shows a blank mind map. (Refer to Appendix C for more information about creating mind maps.)

You'll want to create a blank mind map with "branches" for each of the following categories, as illustrated in Figure 3.1:

- Espoused values
- Artifacts (what you see in the organization)
- Creation story (when applicable, branches from this will also deal with non-profit sector values)
- Survival story
- Hero and heroine stories
- Leadership
- Images

You'll be recording key information on the mind map from the discussion and stories about each of these topics. The information is recorded along the line for that category. Add branches to each category to include more specific information. (Figure 3.2, which appears later in the chapter, shows a filled-in example from HRI.)

Gathering Espoused Values   Espoused values relate to what the organization says about itself. The value doesn't have to be true. These are often aspirational. Ask the group to name or find the organization's espoused values, typically located in statements about core values or in strategic plans. If the values aren't already written down, just ask the group to list the values about which the organization's leadership often talk. Another approach is to share brief stories about accomplishing the organization's mission, and listen for the values underlying

Facilitation Tips

To create the mind map you will need a large roll of paper—we recommend one that is ten feet long and four to six feet wide. Replicate the blank mind map in Figure 3.1. It takes practice to be able to successfully pull out key elements to record on the mind map. If you are concerned about processing the story while pulling key elements, try separating the tasks: elicit the stories by asking questions—see the guiding questions here; take notes and then write down the key elements on the mind map. With practice you'll be able to pull out key elements of stories as you go and record them directly on the mind map. You might also ask different people in the group to listen for the following to help you pull out key elements from the stories:

- Images

- Actual actions taken

- Responses (feelings and actions)

- Descriptive words

the way programs and services are delivered or the way the organization operates. Record these values along the Espoused Values branch of the mind map.

Gathering Artifacts   Artifacts have to do with what you see in the organization. They are found at the surface level of culture and often constitute what people refer to as "our culture"; people may say, "We're a meeting organization; we always have meetings" or "We talk a lot; everyone is allowed to talk." This information is very important to your analysis. Ask the group to describe what they see and feel in the organization. Here are a few specifics to get you going:

- How do people dress?
- What is the office like?
- What kind of professional (and personal) backgrounds do staff and board members have?

Figure 3.1
Blank Mind Map

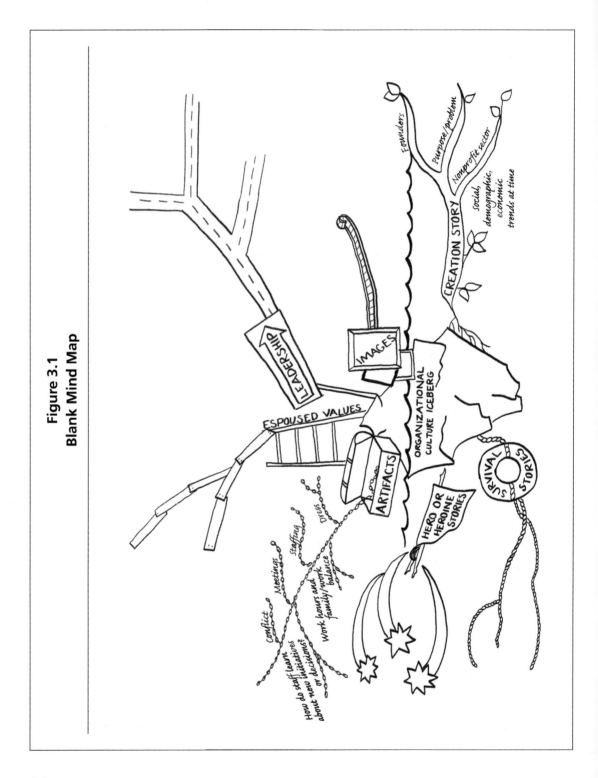

- What kind of experiences do they talk about?
- What kind of people are on the board, and how long do they stay?
- What conflict is visible to staff or observers?
- How is conflict handled?
- How are decisions made?
- What kind of information is valued, sought?
- Who talks in meetings?
- Who follows up on meetings?
- What are processes for accountability?
- What is a "reward" in the organization?
- What is punishment?
- Are there many meetings? What kind?
- Are there agendas, notes?
- What hours do most people work?
- How do you find out about what is happening, about how people feel?
- At what level of formality are relationships and structure?

Facilitation Tips

You can list all these questions on chart paper and list the following headers on the artifacts line of your mind map: work hours, dress, meetings, staff, conflict, decision making, communication, and formality of relationships. After explaining the idea and going over a few examples of answers to the questions listed here, hand out five-by-seven-inch pieces of paper and ask participants to write down one artifact per piece. Add the artifacts people list directly onto your mind map under the appropriate headers.

Storytelling   In this part of the meeting, you'll be asking the group to share stories: the creation story, survival stories, and hero and heroine stories. The next sections list specific questions to help you uncover these stories. As you listen to participants' responses, you will be intuitively drawing on the background information gathered in phase 1 so that you understand what people are saying and can ask follow-up questions. Keep in mind that stories have characters and plots; you should have a sense of a story, a real narrative, by the time people are done telling the stories.

Creation Story Ask the following kinds of questions to help participants tell you the creation story.

- Why was the organization created?
- What was it intended to accomplish?
- Who founded the organization?
- What were the founders' motivations and background?
- What actually happened to form the organization (for example, group meeting and one-person follow-up, merger of other organizations, collaboration, and so on)?
- What was happening in the broader world (social, economic, and demographic trends) at the time?

Survival Story Ask the following kinds of questions to help participants tell you a survival story.

- What was the challenge or threat to the organization?
- Why was it so serious?
- How long ago did the threat arise?
- What was the organization's initial response to the threat?
- Who was leading the response?
- What happened?
- How was the threat ultimately resolved?

At the end of the survival story, ask participants what indications they have that this story endures and is told in the organization repeatedly.

Hero or Heroine Story Ask the following kinds of questions to help participants tell you a hero or heroine story.

- What story or stories are told about past staff when new staff come into the organization?
- What is a story about a staff person that is generally regarded internally as positive (with a smile) and that is told over and over again?
- Is there a story about a particular staff person that seems to show the spark or true nature of the organization?

Once you have found the staff person and story, record the story and ask questions about the person.

- What were they like?
- How did they approach the work, meetings, decisions?
- What is it that makes this staff person appealing as a hero? Why do you think stories continue to be told about this person?

Facilitation Tips

During the storytelling, we recommend that you listen carefully and take many notes, then take a break to summarize key themes from the stories to add to the mind map. As you listen to the stories, explore the meaning of words like _efficient, collaborative, teamwork,_ and so on. For example, when someone says "We survived by collaborating," get the group to tell what was actually done, and record this. Ask questions until responses are clear and specific. Dive deep and repeatedly ask people to say more. Ask "Why?" as much as necessary to unpack the language and hear hidden meanings. If the group seems to get stuck, return to that part of the conversation later.

Probing for Nonprofit Sector Values   Thinking about the creation story of the organization, you can also identify typical nonprofit sector values and why and how those values are operationalized within the organization. You'll be adding these values to a line of the Creation Story branch on the mind map.

Note that this step may not be critical to the objective you are pursuing. If nonprofit sector values do not seem to be important to your objective in describing organizational culture, you could skip this step. However, listing these cultural assumptions will yield a more thorough description of the organization. Because the assumptions suggested by these values may not be critical to your task, you can do this step after the full group meeting.

We suggest that in order to identify these values, you look back at Chapter One to review the theories about why nonprofits exist and the kinds of values about which the organization likely has deep assumptions. You can also refer to Table 1.1, which summarizes the theories and values.

Having refreshed your memory about the theories, consider the creation story and other information about the organization. Which theory or theories about the existence of nonprofits does this organization seem to fit?

Once you have identified the relevant theory or theories, look at the values listed with that theory, think about the stories on the mind map, and try to describe an underlying assumption about each suggested value that is consistent with the stories about the way the organization operates. For example, perhaps the organization is primarily an advocacy organization, so you identify it as fitting into the civic participation and general participation theories. From these you look for assumptions around broad participation and membership in governance, volunteerism, and the way diverse viewpoints within the organization are handled. Perhaps the assumptions are that in order to have a voice in the national political realm, the organization needs to have a large group of active members. At the same time, there is an assumption that decision making needs to happen quickly and that the only way to have a true influence on policy is to take a substantive role in policy discussions, which requires specific and rapid feedback about particular legislative language that is being considered. The second assumption has led to a fairly narrow and quick decision-making process to give timely feedback on legislation, whereas the first assumption has led to a broad request for input once a year on the issues that the organization will address, and an ongoing education campaign with members. These assumptions may put the organization in an ongoing state of tension.

Adding Other Information to the Mind Map There are a couple other categories that you are likely to be able to map once you've finished sharing stories:

- Consider what images came out of the stories, or directly ask about important and typical images in the organization. For example, in this book we have used an iceberg as an image of organizational culture, because only part of the iceberg is exposed and visible, and much of it remains below water and unseen. Another organization uses a person skydiving to represent an image of freedom and self-direction. People may relate the organization or some of the stories to images of a war or of a dance. (This kind of focus on images may not be important or appropriate for some organizations.)

• Consider what characteristics exemplifying good leadership in the organization came up in the stories and record them on the Leadership branch.

Facilitation Tips

Be creative during the meeting. The idea is to get people to share information freely. Here are a couple of ideas about other ways to get people talking.

• Have participants bring photos or images that represent the different categories on the mind map. Put the images on the mind map and talk about why they were chosen. You can add words based on participants' explanations. Be careful with this that the images and words on the mind map are things that resonate with the group as a whole and not just a single person's perspective. Avoid the temptation to include every person's idea out of the sense that every idea has value. The goal here is to uncover the ideas that the _group_ responds to rather than individual ideas. If you need to, you can list everyone's information on one flip-chart and then transfer the ideas held by the group to the mind map.

• Depending on the size of the group, you can break people into smaller groups and have them share stories on one or two of the topics and then pick one or two stories to share with the whole group.

The information yielded during phase 2, step 3 for the Human Rights Institute is summarized in Exhibit 3.3 and resulted in the mind map shown in Figure 3.2. Note that you generally won't write up the narratives (as shown in the exhibit) during these meetings; this is just to give you a sense of what a discussion during the meeting might include.

Figure 3.2
HRI Mind Map

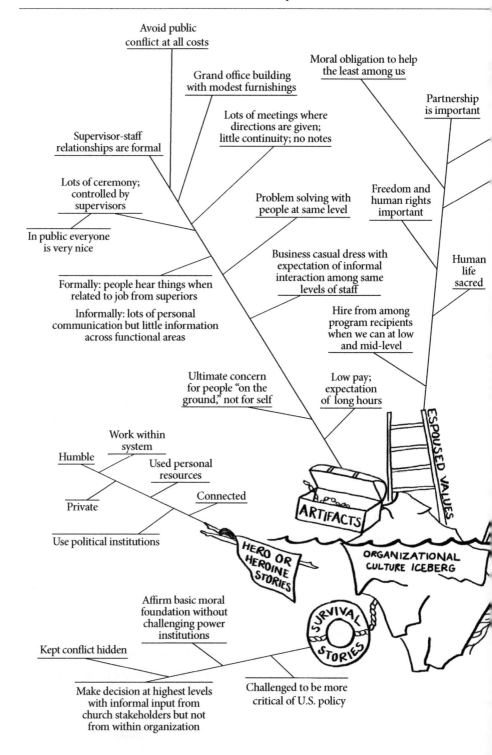

Avoid public
conflict at all costs

Grand office building
with modest furnishings

Moral obligation to help
the least among us

Partnership
is important

Lots of meetings where
directions are given;
little continuity; no notes

Supervisor-staff
relationships are formal

Lots of ceremony;
controlled by
supervisors

Problem solving with
people at same level

Freedom and
human rights
important

In public everyone
is very nice

Business casual dress with
expectation of informal
interaction among same
levels of staff

Human
life
sacred

Formally: people hear things when
related to job from superiors

Informally: lots of personal
communication but little information
across functional areas

Hire from among
program recipients
when we can at low
and mid-level

Ultimate concern
for people "on the
ground," not for self

Low pay;
expectation
of long hours

ESPOUSED VALUES

Work within
system

Humble

Used personal
resources

Connected

Private

ARTIFACTS

Use political institutions

HERO OR
HEROINE
STORIES

ORGANIZATIONAL
CULTURE ICEBERG

Affirm basic moral
foundation without
challenging power
institutions

SURVIVAL
STORIES

Kept conflict hidden

Make decision at highest levels
with informal input from
church stakeholders but not
from within organization

Challenged to be more
critical of U.S. policy

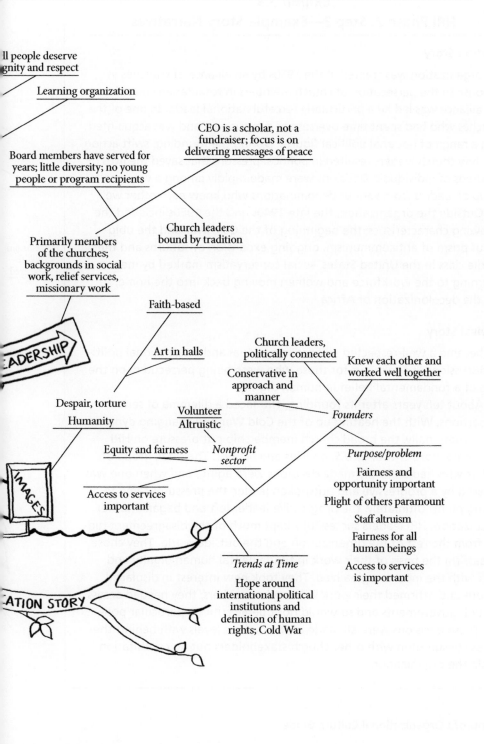

ll people deserve
gnity and respect

Learning organization

CEO is a scholar, not a
fundraiser; focus is on
delivering messages of peace

Board members have served for
years; little diversity; no young
people or program recipients

Church leaders
bound by tradition

Primarily members
of the churches;
backgrounds in social
work, relief services,
missionary work

Faith-based

Art in halls

Church leaders,
politically connected

Knew each other and
worked well together

Conservative in
approach and
manner

LEADERSHIP

Despair, torture

Humanity

Volunteer
Altruistic

Founders

Equity and fairness

*Nonprofit
sector*

Purpose/problem

Fairness and
opportunity important

IMAGES

Access to services
important

Plight of others paramount

Staff altruism

Fairness for all
human beings

Access to services
is important

Trends at Time

Hope around
international political
institutions and
definition of human
rights; Cold War

CREATION STORY

Exhibit 3.3
HRI Phase 2, Step 3—Example Story Narratives

Creation Story

The organization was created in the 1950s by an alliance of churches in response to the persecution of church members in totalitarian countries. The alliance was led by a particularly forceful national leader in one of the churches who had spent time overseas as a missionary and was acquainted with a range of national political figures. During the founding, swift action by a few church leaders resulted in political pressure that saved the lives of hundreds of individuals. Decisions were made rapidly among a very small group of leaders from various denominations who knew each other well.

Outside the organization, the late 1940s and the 1950s included the following characteristics: the beginning of the Cold War and the ubiquitous prism of anticommunism, ongoing expansion of suburbs and the middle class in the United States, social conservatism marked by men returning to the workforce and women moving back into the home, and the decolonization of Africa.

Survival Story

HRI became a well-respected alliance in national and international political discussions. It spoke out for those who were being persecuted, on the basis of a fundamental belief in human dignity.

About ten years after its founding, HRI faced a dilemma of serious proportions. With the heating up of the Cold War and changing dynamics internationally, the broad church membership put pressure on HRI to become more critical of U.S. policies and actions. The small group of leaders who had amicably made decisions were aging, and when one was replaced by a progressive and outspoken leader, the pressures came to a boiling point. Ultimately, the progressive leader left and began another organization. HRI leaders successfully kept much of the disagreement hidden from the rest of the organization and the outside world. They chose to reaffirm the basis of their work in fundamental human dignity and work with the most marginalized. They took new interest in displaced persons and affirmed their work with asylum seekers; they needed access through governments and so would not openly criticize particular policies. These decisions were all made at the highest levels with behind-the-scenes consultation with other church stakeholders but no consultation within the organization.

Hero or Heroine Story

The stories that are told most often are about

- The missionary who flew back to the United States (using her own funds) and passionately testified before Congress about the conditions of people fleeing her adopted country. This testimony resulted in the opening of the asylum process so that more people could enter the United States.

- The soft-spoken original leader who, through his political connections and in quiet dinner meetings, arranged to have hundreds of people airlifted out of a war zone. Staff members from the time said that they didn't even realize he was talking to people to try to resolve the situation. There was angry talk at the offices that the leader was ignoring the human rights crisis. People were up in arms and then the leader suddenly walked in and announced there would be an airlift the next day. Later people realized he had had to keep his connections quiet and work secretively to accomplish the objective.

Espoused Values

Staff members easily list values that the organization publically states as important:

- Human life is sacred.
- Human beings, no matter where they are, have a right to dignity, safety, and opportunity.
- Treat all people with dignity and respect.
- Uphold safety, freedom, and human rights.
- Remain committed to continual learning as an organization.

Even as these values are quickly listed, the group notes that staff members clearly don't feel they are being treated with respect. Illustrations of this in the artifacts are the high turnover, low morale, and deep mistrust of the organization's senior management and leadership, as expressed in a recent staff survey.

There is also some skepticism about the commitment to continual learning. The facilitator notes this and informs the group that they will be coming back to these inconsistencies.

(continued)

Exhibit 3.3 *(continued)*

Artifacts

Generally around offices, people are friendly, dressed business casual, and are expected to talk with one another about family, recent trips, or hobbies prior to engaging in serious dialogue.

Conflict is never seen in the open. If there is conflict, it is handled behind closed doors, and no one hears what happened or what the outcome is unless it directly affects his or her job.

Staff members vary significantly in their backgrounds, with many of the lower and a few mid-level staff having received some support or services from the organization or churches affiliated with the organization. Upper management and most of middle management have a background in social services but have not received services.

There are lots of formal meetings, but that is not where ideas are generated or problems solved. Meetings are places for distributing information. At the middle level, problem solving happens somewhat spontaneously in the halls. Senior-level management holds its own meetings where there may be problem solving and discussion.

There are limited formal notes written and distributed from meetings. Staff members are expected to find out on their own what happened if they were not able to attend. There is not always consistency from one meeting to the next in terms of referring to what happened in earlier meetings.

People work long hours for little pay and are engaged because they care about the work. Senior management assumes this attitude as a given—that is, it is an expectation. Complaints about salaries or hours are likely to be met with skepticism about commitment.

The overall space is grand in scale, with modest furnishings and significant art and faith-related artifacts. The office building is a community landmark.

Members of senior management all have private offices with windows as well as ample work and meeting space. This is a perk of leadership. Most other HRI staff work in cubicles with little or no privacy; this makes informal interaction easy, but concentration, which seems to be increasingly required, difficult. Many cubicles are designed with work areas facing inward so that staff members cannot see who is walking by their space.

The table in Exhibit 3.4 summarizes some of the key nonprofit sector theories that are relevant to HRI, and examines HRI's stories for underlying assumptions predicted by the theories.

Phase 2, Step 4: Analyze Our Stories and Reveal Hidden Truths in the Culture   In this step, you analyze the information you have just gathered. The purpose of analyzing the mind map is to identify common themes (ideas and concepts). Understanding these themes allows you to formulate underlying assumptions that describe core elements of the organization's culture. These themes should have real power and meaning; they carry the context of the stories

Exhibit 3.4
HRI Nonprofit Theories and Values

General Theories About Nonprofit Existence	Underlying Assumptions
Public good orientation	• There is a deep belief in equity and fairness, and that the world should be a fair place for human beings. People's ability to survive and succeed should not be fundamentally tied to where they were born or their countries' leadership. • Access to services is important. • There are few limitations on who can receive help from the organization because all human life is sacred.
Voluntary, charity	• Staff members are selected in part from former clients of the organization in order to "give them a chance" to improve their circumstances. • Personal conflict or issues are not important in comparison to the plight of others. • Staff generally should work here because they have a deep moral sense of what is right and not because they expect significant monetary returns. • There is a spiritual faith basis to the work—we are morally obligated to help those less fortunate than ourselves.

> **Exhibit 3.5**
> **HRI Themes**
>
> A few of the themes identified by HRI are as follows:
>
> - Small leadership circle
> - Partnership with government entities; conflict avoidance
> - Connection to religious institutions
> - Humility
> - Serious work environment

recorded on your mind map. In addition to identifying themes, you can also use your analysis to identify inconsistencies in beliefs and actual experiences.

Identifying Themes In this method, staff use the mind map to help them remember the details of the story and look for commonalities or themes—ideas, concepts, words, images, or actions that come up more than once or twice. You will then record these themes on chart paper. Exhibit 3.5 lists themes identified by HRI.

Facilitation Tips

Have everyone look at the mind map silently for a few minutes. Remind them that the mind map is there to help them remember the details of the story—so if they remember something and it isn't quoted exactly on the mind map, that is okay. Participants should be looking for concepts, words, images, actions, or ideas that come up in multiple places. As people look for themes, you might suggest various perspectives from which to consider the drawing:

- Reflect on the language that was used in stories.

- Think about what part of the stories got people excited, where there was energy in the telling and listening to the story.

- Consider the kinds of things that happened in the story and the way people described them.

- Uncover the commonalities among the key people who show up in the mind map.

- Look for images or metaphors that were used more than once. Are they positive or negative; do they hold anything in common?

Record the themes that people identify. Make sure that the group (in general) sees the commonality or agrees that the theme is accurate. When you record the theme, it will be easier for you later if you title it with one word. For example, the group may identify a sense of fun or playfulness that runs through the hero story and the survival stories. They may also see that images that come up and resonate are silly and that the relationships among staff are jesting without being too personal. You might name this theme *fun-loving*.

Identifying Inconsistencies Using this method, you look for areas where what the organization says (its espoused values) directly contradicts or significantly differs from what actually happens at the organization. Schein notes that such discrepancies usually indicate that there's a deeper assumption at work. Consequently, by identifying these inconsistencies, we know the kind of behavior that the assumption is driving and therefore something about the assumption itself. Further, as action science theories and dialectic change theories highlight, bringing to light the conflict between espoused theories (what is said) and theories in action (what is done) can be a significant first step in creating change (Argyris, 1996, 1997; Fernandez and Rainey, 2006). By making this dissonance conscious, you can create the first impetus toward change or realignment. You should record any inconsistencies and hold on to them. You will seek underlying assumptions that explain them during the next step. Exhibit 3.6 describes two inconsistencies identified at HRI.

Phase 2, Step 5: Describe Your Organization's Culture and Its Broad Benefits and Risks In this step, which may require additional facilitator preparation and consequently a separate meeting, you draft a short description of your organization's core cultural elements and do a preliminary analysis of benefits and risks associated with those elements given the current environment. Generally you'll prepare the short description of organizational culture using the

Facilitation Tips

You might ask the group these questions:

- How do the espoused values and artifacts on the mind map compare? Where are they consistent or inconsistent?

- How do the espoused values and behaviors compare? Where are they consistent or inconsistent?

- How do the espoused values and the stories of survival and heroism compare?

At this point you simply need to name these inconsistencies and record them on a sheet. For example, an organization may espouse collaboration as a value, and management may say they want to collaborate, but none of the big successes and little other work is actually done collaboratively. In fact, the organization excels, has a particular drive for results, and revels in its independence. In this case you might name this inconsistency *collaboration and independence*, but remember that it has a deep explanation behind it.

Exhibit 3.6
HRI Inconsistencies

The most significant inconsistencies identified in the HRI discussion are as follows:

Internal and external dignity. The espoused belief in human dignity is not consistent within the organization. Staff feel that dignity for them would include respect for their opinions, yet such respect is not shown.

Internal and external conflict. The way the organization approaches conflict externally in the international realm and the way conflict is dealt with inside the organization differ dramatically. Externally the organization is willing to "fight" for people who are being tortured or persecuted, but internally conflict is not allowed, not seen, and not discussed.

---

techniques described in the following sections prior to a meeting. You'll review and analyze the benefits and risks with the group.

With practice and intuition, you'll be able to review the list of themes and inconsistencies and draft a set of underlying assumptions that describe core elements of the organization's culture. This process requires an intuitive leap that becomes easier as you develop more of a cultural perspective. When you have the description right, people in the organization are likely to agree that it does indeed paint an accurate picture. (It is worth noting that sometimes this agreement won't be forthcoming, particularly in a group. If the cultural description is controversial, it may take time for the organization to embrace it fully.) But more important, the description will accurately explain why the organization's behavior seems contradictory or confusing. The following steps and table will help you identify underlying assumptions. Keep in mind that over time—as experience feeds your intuition—you may not need all these steps.

We're going to use three approaches to draft underlying assumptions (sometimes also called core beliefs) that will form the heart of your description of culture: using themes, explaining inconsistencies (in artifacts and beliefs), and reviewing nonprofit sector background.

Using Themes   First, look explicitly at the themes identified during the previous step. Use Table 3.1, Organizational Culture Theme Analysis, which identifies areas where there are often important organizational cultural assumptions operating. (These are listed in the left column.) The top part of the left column asks questions about observed artifacts and behaviors; the bottom part names common areas where there are underlying assumptions operating. The remaining columns (and you can add as many as necessary) are where you list the major themes you've identified.

To use the table, label the columns with your themes, then ask, Does the theme suggest anything about the topic in row 1, in row 2, in row 3, and so on? Themes will not have something to say about every row. Ultimately you will use the table as guidance to write a few sentences that describe the deep underlying assumptions about your organizational culture. When the words feel right and the image is clear and the assumptions help explain the way the organization behaves, then you have captured some of the core elements of your organization's culture. Exhibit 3.7 shows HRI's analysis of its cultural themes.

Table 3.1
Organizational Culture Theme Analysis

Artifacts and Behaviors	Theme X	Theme Y	(Add more themes as needed)
How do people interact and connect with one another—friendly, as family, professionally, cordially? Who is an insider? Who is an outsider, and why?			
How do people work together in your organization? How do people organize to get things done?			
What kinds of rewards are given for work well done?			
What punishment is dealt out if work is poor? Who decides what work is poor quality?			
Use of information: What kind of information is considered valid, and what makes it valid? How does information flow or move?			
How do procedures change within the organization?			
What is necessary to get results in the outside world?			
How do people learn about new ideas in the field?			
How is the organization structured, and how important is structure to the organization?			
Policies and practices: What kind, how thorough, how explicit, how important are they?			

Decision making: What is needed to make a decision, and who makes it?			
Deep Assumptions			
Human nature: Are humans inherently good or bad? Is transformation possible?			
Relationship to our environment: Can humans control or harness the environment?			

Revisiting Nonprofit Theories and Values   You will want to revisit the larger nonprofit themes that you identified in phase 2, step 3 ("Probing for Nonprofit Sector Values"). Pull out that description and keep it in mind as you prepare to write your cultural description. (See Table 1.1 for a general description of the nonprofit sector theories and values and see Exhibit 3.1 for a description of HRI's specific nonprofit background.)

Explaining Inconsistencies   A final approach to drafting assumptions is to look at the inconsistencies that you identified from your stories. Consider these inconsistencies in light of the organization's history and the information about assumptions you've begun to gather from analyzing themes and from the nonprofit sector theories and values. You should see underlying assumptions that explain the inconsistencies. If there is an inconsistency that doesn't seem to be explained or addressed, then you may want to spend a few minutes brainstorming about the kind of underlying assumption that may be causing the inconsistency. Exhibit 3.8 describes HRI's explanation for its inconsistencies.

Writing the Culture Description   With the information from these approaches and analyzing the material you've gathered, you should be able to summarize a few core cultural elements. These elements are at the deepest level of culture—the underlying assumptions, sometimes referred to as core beliefs. Start with the notes that you've made on your tables. Take these hints and draft a series of statements that describe deeply held assumptions and beliefs that appear to be

Exhibit 3.7

How HRI Describes Its Cultural Themes

Artifacts and Behaviors	Small Leadership Circle	Partnership with Government Agencies; Conflict Avoidance	Connection to Religious Institutions	Humility	Serious Work Environment
How do people interact and connect with one another—friendly, as family, professionally, cordially? Who is an insider? Who is outsider, and why?	Leaders have the wisdom. There are levels of "insiders" within senior management; important external and church stakeholders are the "most inside."	Follow rules.	Those within the religious frame are generally insiders in terms of behavior but not in terms of input.	Don't claim credit.	Staff are expected to care about one another, ask about one another, and always be aware of the plight of others.
How do people work together in your organization? How do people organize to get things done?	Leaders should make big decisions because they have knowledge and connections. Staff should implement ideas when told to do so.	Draw little attention to yourself. Personal disagreements are irrelevant.	Draw on hierarchy of religious institutions.	It's the work that matters, not recognition of you in it.	Horrific images of torture and persecution abound and act as motivators for work.
What kinds of rewards are given for work well done?			Rewards are in heaven.		

Question				
What punishment is dealt out if work is poor? Who decides what work is poor quality?				
Use of information: What kind of information is considered valid, and what makes it valid? How does information flow or move?	Information flows down; organization responds immediately when life is threatened; on-the-ground information is of highest value.		Draw on missionaries and other religious venues to gather information about on-the-ground circumstances.	
How do procedures change within organization? What is necessary to get results in the outside world? How do people learn about new ideas in the field?	If policies change within the organization, that must come from the top. Management uses political institutions and connections to get results. You should draw on personal on-the-ground experiences to learn.	It is difficult to change organization or inter-organization processes. Conflict is counterproductive in seeking change.	Religious frame is prescriptive and slow to change, and it limits information sharing.	We need a clear, well-thought-out rationale for decision making.

(continued)

Exhibit 3.7 (continued)

Artifacts and Behaviors	Small Leadership Circle	Partnership with Government Agencies; Conflict Avoidance	Connection to Religious Institutions	Humility	Serious Work Environment
How is the organization structured, and how important is structure to the organization?	Hierarchy.	Work in silos based on funding.			
Policies and practices: What kind, how thorough, how explicit, how important are they?					
Decision making: What is needed to make a decision, and who makes it?	Decisions are made quickly during crises.	To do something different requires a lot of rationale and justification.	Decisions must be rooted in moral arguments.		

Deep Assumptions			
Human nature: Are humans inherently good or bad? Is transformation possible?	Transformation comes from doing good and following the rules.	People can be good.	Beware of pride.
Relationship to our environment: Can humans control or harness the environment?		God through Christ will guide the way. God is ultimately in control of the world and environment. The organization shouldn't focus on changing or controlling the environment, although stewardship of the environment may be important.	Be compassionate, welcoming, and hopeful.
We have limited ability to impact the environment.			

Exhibit 3.8
How HRI Explains Its Inconsistencies

In the case of HRI, the first inconsistency had to do with human dignity and an apparent lack of respect for internal staff opinions, along with a definite disinterest in participatory decision making. In light of the assumptions around leadership and the connection to the religious institutions, this inconsistency seems less strange. The need for quick decision making in crisis and the hierarchical habits of critically important participating religious institutions mean that staff participation is less important and may even be seen as the "wrong" way to get things done.

The second inconsistency was related to internal and external conflict. Given the underlying assumption that leadership has the knowledge and connections and *should* make decisions and the belief that working within political institutions and with government systems is the right way to create change, it makes sense that internal conflict would be frowned on. After all, internal conflict would tend to weaken the bargaining position of leadership as it went external. Combine these assumptions with a belief in the importance of quick action, and there is a general dampening of motivation to create good systems and habits for dealing with conflict. Finally, the hierarchical habits of leadership and the founding stakeholders would naturally lead to a view of internal conflict as a sign of disrespect for authority, elders, and rules.

---

driving the behavior of the organization. You may title the beliefs so that they are summarized and easy to refer to.

Here's an example of a deeply held assumption to help you get started:

A small group of high-level people can make decisions quickly and accurately and can draw on political connections without publicity. Because human life is so precious, when lives are threatened this speed is critical.

Generally, you'll want to complete this brief summary of deep assumptions in preparation for a second meeting with the organizational culture team.

Analyzing Risks and Benefits The risks and benefits of your organization's culture are likely to become obvious as you describe the culture. After writing up the cultural description, do a quick initial analysis of the risks and benefits associated with it. (Exhibit 3.9 is HRI's description of its culture, risks, and benefits.)

Exhibit 3.9
How HRI Describes Its Culture, Risks, and Benefits

The result of the analysis of themes and inconsistencies for the Human Rights Institute follows.

HRI Organizational Culture Summary

We have two guiding assumptions:

1. *Human dignity.* Because all people are created by God and in his image, all people deserve to be treated with dignity and given an opportunity to fulfill their calling.

2. *Obligation to improve the world.* We, as people of faith, have an obligation to help those less fortunate than ourselves.

Our Core Beliefs

1. **Quick decisions save human lives, and hierarchical structures allow this speed.** A small group of high-level people can make decisions quickly and accurately (they have the knowledge) and can draw on political connections without publicity. Because human life is so precious, when lives are threatened this speed is critical, and taking time for broader input and participation might threaten this speed. Further, any integration and cross-departmental communication is likely to make it harder to act quickly. HRI was founded and initially wholly funded by religious bodies whose history and practices have reflected a strong, hierarchical leadership and decision-making style. The ongoing engagement of these religious institutions is critical to the organization.

2. **The most effective way to effect change is to influence levers of power by working within the system.** Those in the system have the power and resources to make change. We can influence those people through personal political connections and congressional testimony. If we damage these relationships, then we will not be able to effect change and help those in need.

3. **Services to persons fleeing persecution or entering the United States are important but secondary to influencing the power structure.** Service providers are important once those in power have made decisions.

4. **"The work" is important.** People should perform this work based on moral imperatives and a desire to do good. They should not expect

(continued)

Exhibit 3.9 *(continued)*

significant monetary or other rewards. Further, the work improving the lives of the "least among us" is where our resources should go, not toward the operation of bureaucracy.

5. **Conflict has no place in this work.** Public conflict is detrimental to exercising influence and to motivating caregivers. Personal conflict is irrelevant to the larger issues, and any legitimate conflict about the work will be handled behind closed doors.

6. **We want to give people an opportunity to work because it is a way to fulfill the need for human dignity.** We hire individuals who have received our services or services from our religious affiliates when we can.

Initial Analysis of Our Culture

Having identified core beliefs that are at the heart of the behavior of our organization, we completed a preliminary analysis of the broad benefits and risks of these beliefs in the context of what HRI wanted to achieve.

Core Belief	Benefits of Core Belief	Risks of Core Belief
Speedy decisions save lives.	We want to respond rapidly.	We limit information gathering and sharing.
There is an appropriate way to effect change.	We are able to influence key decision makers.	Only a few people are qualified to do this; we emphasize their role and not the role of others; what management does doesn't matter to other staff.
Services are secondary.	This belief provides focus and clarity about priorities. It is most important to get people out of the horrible situation and then provide services.	Direct service providers feel less important and less a part of the success.
The work is important.	We are committed to doing authentic work that makes a difference in people's lives.	Pay low salaries—at least it's something, and it doesn't take money from "the work"; staff don't have wisdom to share. There are lost efficiencies and knowledge because different areas recreate information instead of sharing it.

| Conflict has no place in this work. | We want to be peaceful. | We avoid all conflict by controlling it—don't let it happen. We miss out on creative resolution of conflicts that can result in improved processes and mission outcomes. |
| We must give people opportunities to work. | Hiring former clients shows a commitment to our core belief in human dignity; it is a means of "walking the walk." | Many lower-level and some mid-level staff feel unable to question the authority of senior management because of the sense that the job was "given" to them. |

You can do this in preparation for a meeting or with the participants in the meeting. Here is an example of such an analysis:

We believe, and experience has proven, that a small group of high-level people can make decisions quickly and accurately and can draw on political connections without publicity. Because human life is so precious, when lives are threatened this speed is critical. These are clear and proven benefits. However, this approach to our work can alienate staff and other stakeholders who do not understand the reasons for our quick, authoritative approach, who feel that their opinions are not valued, and who feel that they do not receive the level of dignity we promise them. Furthermore, the approach has proven to limit career paths into positions of authority in our organization, and may be a cause for our high turnover.

Facilitation Tip

You may choose to end the second meeting after this preliminary analysis to give participants a chance to reflect on the information you've gathered. You can end the meeting with a single question to everyone present: What have you learned about our culture today that you are taking away with you?

Phase 3: Assess Implications for the Objective and Your Plan

In this phase, you are focused on internalizing what you've learned about your organization's culture, understanding its impact on what you are trying to achieve, and completing action plans.

Phase 3, Step 1: Review the Objective   Review the objective for examining organizational culture that you identified with top management and at the beginning of your group discussion. Make sure that the objective still makes sense and is as specific as possible.

Phase 3, Step 2: Understand the Implications   In this step, you consider your organizational culture in terms of how it can help or hinder work toward the specific objective. Make a list of the answers to the following questions:

- What aspects of our organizational culture (beliefs, benefits, and risks) will help us achieve our objective? How can we use this information in action planning?

- What aspects of our organizational culture will hinder us in achieving the objective? How can we use this information in action planning?

The answers to these questions will be the source of ideas or helpful hints about planning your actions to address your objective. Remember that shifting or changing elements of organizational culture requires intentional small steps that are a response to the deepest parts the culture. The ideas or helpful hints are suggestive of important things to build into your action plan and are likely to make you more successful in achieving your objective. In the next step, you'll take this information and create a plan of action. Exhibit 3.10 summarizes the results of steps 1 and 2 at HRI.

Phase 3, Step 3: Create Your Action Plan   In this step, you apply your understanding of your organization's culture and how it impacts your objective to drafting a specific action plan.

For some organizations, this may mean focusing more on what is good and valuable in the culture and finding ways to make those parts of the culture more dominant. Other organizations may be changing some of the artifacts of culture, adopting different values, or creating entirely new underlying assumptions to frame the organization's work. Artifacts are the easiest to change. In contrast,

Exhibit 3.10
HRI Objective and Implications

Objective: to reduce middle management turnover. The first step is to give middle managers a sense of appropriate engagement with senior management in a way that does not compromise speed of decision making in a crisis. Communication should be characterized as

- Open (where both sides are able to raise issues and have discussion)
- Regular (at least once a week)
- Mutually respectful (no personalization of issues; serious consideration of others' perspectives and ideas)

HELP What about our organizational culture will HELP us achieve our objective?	ACTION IMPLEMENTATION How could this knowledge help with action planning?
Belief in small teams and quick decisions	Begin with a small team that has advocacy experience and find something to be successful with quickly.
Belief in hierarchical structure with senior management in charge	Get senior management buy-in early; the leadership position of senior management needs to be valued in the process.
Desire to influence power centers and not risk these relationships	Review action plans with our major sources of funding so that the plans do not threaten key government relationships.
Belief in the importance of the work	Frame actions in terms of how they can positively influence people who are being tortured, persecuted, and displaced. This is a positive motivator to senior management.
Avoidance of conflict	Engage in mutually respectful dialogue to avoid conflict.

(continued)

Exhibit 3.10 *(continued)*

HINDER What about our organizational culture will HINDER us in achieving this objective?	ACTION IMPLEMENTATION How could this knowledge help with action planning?
Ultimate belief that speed and a small group of leaders making decisions are most effective	Look for ways to facilitate a quick turnaround.
Existing hierarchy and comfort with this structure	Build in a step for senior management to give input to any group working on the issue and for senior management to be engaged in distributing conclusions and recommendations from the work group to the rest of staff.
Little belief in need for integration and information sharing	Don't include broad distribution of notes from meetings or process; horizontal sharing of information shouldn't be the first step.

new deep underlying assumptions could take years to become part of the organizational culture.

As you do action planning, be very clear and specific. For example, don't say, "We want more teamwork"; say, "The finance department and the staff operating housing services will meet on a regular basis, share information, and put in place new mechanisms to make sure emergency loans are given out within one week of the time people apply." Don't say, "We want the public to recognize our value"; say, "We want the stories of our compassionate, caring staff and the results we have achieved to be visible to leaders in our community." You will need to describe specifically what you want to have happen, whether it is a change in artifacts (for example, processes, types of meetings) or the addition of a new underlying assumption.

You'll also want to be very precise about the role that core beliefs and underlying assumptions of your organizational culture are playing in achieving the objective and what you will do about that role. For example, let's assume there is a core belief that success is dependent on being good partners with others in the community and a belief that too much visibility will make it difficult to obtain partners. However, in the current environment, the organization needs to communicate its successes, and those core beliefs hinder efforts to get success stories out to the public. The organization might choose to use these beliefs to its advantage and create a *joint* communication strategy that puts out success stories about the organization and its partners. In this case, the organization is not changing an assumption. Rather, it is changing some artifacts by changing some communication protocols. It may also need to create a new belief about the value and importance of communication skills in the organization—which will occur as the new protocols generate success, reinforcing the new belief.

For each shift or change, whether it is to an artifact or a core belief, you'll need to answer the following questions. Keep in mind the information from your chart of what could help and what could hinder action planning and that you want to draw on elements already in the culture whenever you can.

- What specific actions will be taken and when?
- Who will be responsible for actions?
- How will we know if this element of our culture has been changed, altered, or eliminated or if the new artifacts that we are pursuing are in place?
- Who will specifically check on actions and their results, and when will that be done?
- How will we measure whether the change is actually addressing our objective?

Note: An actual action plan would, of course, include actions and due dates. We assume that you are familiar with how to create an action plan, so Exhibit 3.11 focuses on the approach HRI would follow in developing the plan, rather than the plan itself.

Phase 4: Define Intentional Action and Implementation Plan

Finally, you must gather the necessary resources and internal support to implement your plans. Implementation entails making changes that can threaten people's comfort. People fear failure; inertia seems to be not only a physical law but a psychological one, as does the notion that making changes requires more energy and usually more time than does staying the same.

As you move into implementation, keep in mind that people need motivation to change. They need to understand why and how to change, and they need

Exhibit 3.11
HRI Action Plan Approach

For HRI, there is a significant question about whether senior management believes the analysis that a reduction in turnover among middle management is critical to the organization. Nevertheless, we would recommend the following approach to HRI's management.

Management should create a small task force that includes senior leaders, mid-level managers, and program staff to work on a very specific issue related to the well-being of torture victims in a particular country. The purpose of this small task force is to come up with a few short-term actions that can be implemented by the organization and that are highly likely to result in visible success. The task force must engage all its members and must address behavior that in the past has made staff members feel a lack of respect. In this way, the task force functions as a microcosm that is not focused on an abstract idea of better communication. It is focused on a particular problem that can be addressed by improved communication.

The task force itself will have the power to implement these changes without further input from senior management. The task force and the remainder of senior management will announce the implementation of these changes. The task force will gather data about the impact of the changes and communicate them first to the remainder of senior management and then, with senior management, to the rest of the organization. As the changes demonstrate success, the task force and senior management will highlight the importance of true staff participation, beyond senior management, in this process.

The objectives are (1) to create, over time, a new belief that cross-level discussion and planning that is truly valued by senior management can be effective in solving problems and (2) to reinforce behaviors of open, regular, and respectful communication.

With this success and a new belief that internal communication does not necessarily slow down decision making, the task force could choose another specific issue to resolve with increased communication. Or it could hold a more general conversation about what specific behaviors might need to change across the organization in order to have open, regular, and respectful communication among different levels of staff. For example, the number of meetings involving only senior management would be reduced and, in their place, meetings would be held that include program managers and staff, with the chair or presiding role rotating among all levels and members; with regard to respect for all staff members, a change might include identifying words or behaviors that signal a lack of respect to staff. Having identified these recommended actions, the task force (and organization) could set up ways to practice the new behaviors.

nonthreatening, nonjudgmental ways to practice those changes. Your action plan should take these needs into consideration.

There are many different theories about change and how to implement it. It's not our purpose here to deeply review this literature; further, we'd note that often the best change methodology or theory is dependent on the experiences of the organization and the people leading the shifts. Organizations typically have methods they have successfully used in the past to make changes or implement and monitor action plans. (For more on change processes, see Schein, 1999, and Gallos, 2006, pp. 94–126).

Instead of focusing on the details of a particular method of change, we'll review a few characteristics of implementation that we believe are important in making the shifts, additions, or changes last—making them stick.

Leadership   First and foremost, leadership matters. Leaders matter as creators and evolvers of culture, and they matter because if they resist changing organizational culture at *any* level, then change will be nearly impossible. Although he was not speaking specifically about nonprofit organizations, Schein claims that the essential function of leadership is the manipulation of culture. In fact, he says, "The only thing of importance that leaders do is create and manage culture," and "The unique talent of leaders is the ability to understand and work within culture" (2004, p. 5).

Without a doubt, founding and longtime leaders have a profound impact on the culture in their organizations. Because organizational culture begins with the first groups of people addressing the organization's first challenges, and this founding group bases these approaches on their values, founders and their assumptions and values live long past their terms as leaders. Further, founding leaders are particularly powerful creators of culture because it is their passion that convinces others to financially support a vision without the promise of financial reward.

In observing many nonprofit organizations, we noted that often, more than any single factor, leaders are shapers of organizational culture. It is from leaders that others see what an organization *truly* values—rather than what it *claims* it values. It is from leaders that others understand what is acceptable and what is not. It is from leaders that others learn which behaviors are rewarded and which are not. Peter Brinckerhoff expressed it this way during our interview with him: "People don't always understand the difference between behavior and culture. Talk without behavior is not culture. If leadership models behavior, it becomes part of the culture." Thus, in understanding leadership's role in creating and evolving culture, you can see that leaders must commit to the action plan that has been developed and, further, must visibly demonstrate support for that plan if it is to succeed.

Heifetz and Linsky (2002) tell us it's not change that people resist as much as loss—or the perception of loss. "Exercising leadership involves helping organizations and communities figure out what, and whom, they are willing to let go. Of all the values honored by the community, which of them can be sacrificed in the interest of progress?" (p. 94).

In each of the cases we discussed in Chapter Two, you can see the unique role leaders played in trying to guide their organization through challenges. Those who had an intuitive sense of the organization's culture, such as Amy Ginsburg at Manna Food Center, Jaime Alvarado at Somos Mayfair, and Steven McCullough at Bethel New Life, appeared to be having more success at the time we interviewed them.

Further, leaders who are reflective can be helpful in implementing action plans focused on change. This is particularly true if you are operating at the deep levels of culture—shifting or adding assumptions and beliefs. Several change models suggest that managers and leaders need to be confronted with the juxtaposition of their desires and espoused beliefs and their actual history and behavior. The ensuing cognitive dissonance motivates them to change. However, particularly in cases where leadership has played at least a tacit, if not active, role in the perpetuation of the belief, the leader also needs to be reflective. The leader must have the ability and willingness to examine his or her motivations and behaviors and be open to discovering personal blind spots. Much of the leadership literature today discusses the need for reflection and for authenticity. Organizations where leaders are unable or unwilling to be reflective about the culture and their specific contributions to it are unlikely to make and sustain beneficial culture shifts. A leader's willingness to look deeply at his or her beliefs and behaviors and how these affect others is essential to making shifts in organizational culture.

Leaders and organizational culture engage in an interactive and responsive dance. Leaders, particularly early leaders, do contribute many of their personal assumptions to the organization's culture, but the organization and its experiences can shift and change these assumptions over time. Further, because culture is a conservative force that sets limits and boundaries for behavior, new leaders coming into the organization are just as limited as anyone else. They must understand the boundaries if they are to succeed in shifting them.

Group Process   A second important factor in making learning stick is to recognize that the group process you used to determine the key elements of organizational culture and create your plan marks the beginning, not the end, of interactions with groups across the organization. As Kurt Lewin, the father of social psychology and action research, pointed out, "The group to which an individual belongs is the ground for his perceptions, his feelings and his actions" (1948, p. vii). Clearly groups must be the focus of change, which is why we involve groups in culture assessment and implementing plans around organizational culture.

Lewin went on to point out, as have many others after him, that participation in the decisions, in the feedback about results, and in the ongoing adjustments to the plan is necessary to create motivation and momentum for implementation. You'll need to make sure that groups across the organization understand and have participated in the process of action planning. Perhaps even more important, make sure that these groups have access to the data and information that show that the plan is working or not working.

Feedback Loops   Your action plan must contain specifically identified points for testing the results of implementation against the desired results, and time for reflection on this information. These reflection points are known as feedback loops, another key component of many change models, particularly those that address learning organizations. If you establish times to stop to review how things are going, you make it more likely that the review will actually occur, people in the organization will take the implementation more seriously, and everyone is more likely to sustain the new behaviors rather than revert to old ones or simply stop trying.

Storytelling, Myth Making, and Celebrating Success   A fourth component of implementation should be storytelling or myth making. Remember that culture is ultimately about creating meaning amid uncertainty, and that stories and myths are people's narrative ways of conveying meaning. You should find ways to create new stories that help support the action plan, and listen for stories that others are telling. Keep in mind that the stories need to be based on something real and true, something with which people in the organization will identify. How do you create new stories? Look and listen for interesting characters in the organization who epitomize the results you are seeking. Tell stories about their trials and how they overcame them. Have other people share stories about the success of implementation.

Don't forget to celebrate success. As Schein said in a recent interview, "We want to do things to the culture and that doesn't work. Culture is the end product of learning, so what you have to do is create new business practices that are more successful than what you had before. When that occurs, employees will gradually adopt the values and assumptions of those practices" (Weiss, 2008). Ultimately success is the best reinforcer of the cultural changes you seek, so you want everyone in the organization to share in it.

Innovative Ways to Create and Try On New Organizational Culture Beliefs and Behaviors   Leaders can intentionally create opportunities for new beliefs and behaviors to develop. For example, they can hire newcomers and intentionally focus discussion around their experiences, or they can create opportunities for staff teams to try on new beliefs in a safe context. In the next two sections, we discuss innovative ways to try on new beliefs and behaviors.

Experiential Training and Natural Challenges   Experiential training draws on research showing that if a person experiences a change, idea, or concept with her entire body, she is more likely to remember it and incorporate the learning. Two innovative examples of experiential training models are the use of outdoor activities, such as rappelling, climbing mountains, or completing ropes courses, and equine-assisted growth and learning, which uses the sensitivity of horses to help reflect group dynamics. Both of these models use experiences outside the normal workplace to help illustrate and reflect on group behavior and individuals' mental models. A trained facilitator can design specific outdoor or equine-assisted activities that will bring out deep elements of the group's culture. Further, in processing these experiences, the facilitator can help the group identify concrete behaviors to reinforce. Finally, in follow-up activities, the group can practice these behaviors to help solidify them. In this way, staff can quickly identify core beliefs and understand how they affect behavior and can identify specific examples of new behaviors that they would like to see in the workplace.

For example, imagine that an organization holds a strong cultural belief about quick decision making and saving lives, and further, a belief that broad participation slows down that decision making. We might design a rescue scenario that would be hard for one small group to solve quickly. A team from this organization might "fail" in this rescue scenario; then another team with broader input or different groups trying different approaches might succeed. From this exercise, we could focus in the debrief on the role that broad-based participation played in solving the problem. Staff could explore which behaviors allowed that participation, which behaviors shut it down, and how behaviors related to success. After defining new behaviors they'd like to try, they could try the rescue again and practice the behaviors. This kind of practice in a safe, nonwork space can create a credible and important bridge in helping people change. (For more ideas, see www.ThinkOutside.net.)

Professional Coaching   Coaching is built around questioning, listening, appreciative discovery, and constructive feedback. It focuses on heightening trust in what one knows and identifying where one needs to stretch to sustain or improve individual or organization performance. Through a series of dynamic conversations, either one-on-one or with teams or groups, a coach supports organization leaders over time in examining their deepest beliefs about their organizations and their management and leadership, imagining shifts in those beliefs, designing actions to carrying out selected shifts, and actually implementing the shifts and fine-tuning the strategies. Professional coaches can support organization leaders and teams or groups for an unlimited period to sustain innovation and new learning.

Ultimately, the success of any approach to "making it stick" requires openness, commitment to trying new things and making shifts, willingness to practice and learn, and explicit dedication of human and financial resources to the effort.

CLOSING THOUGHTS

The time and resources devoted to the ROC may seem initially overwhelming. However, once you've completed this process one time, you can use the description of your organization's culture repeatedly in management decisions, communication, formulating strategy, understanding how to ensure action on plans, and so on. We discuss these examples further in Chapter Five. Furthermore, you can designate people within the organization as the "keepers" of organizational culture or define particular times in the organization's regular processes to review organizational culture, which will ensure that culture is considered as the organization moves forward.

We look forward over the next several years to hearing about your experiences using the ROC process and to further refining this tool. We believe that in times of economic peril and growing human hardship, when nonprofit organizations are expected more than ever to do more good with fewer resources, knowing the hidden truths of organizational culture will provide an invaluable tool for nonprofit leaders and capacity builders. And the truth shall set you free: discovering the hidden truths of organizational culture offers a new opportunity to free nonprofits from the stress of failed change efforts so that more resources—human as well as fiscal—will be available to enhance the quality of human and community life throughout our society and the world.

Chapter FOUR

Reflections on Organizational Culture

We assume that you are reading this book because you care about non-profit organizations and their ability to succeed—to make a difference for their target clients, constituents, and communities. We hope you now agree that curiosity about organizational culture needs to be an integral part of how you envision and pursue organizational success. Whether you are an executive director or CEO, program manager or supervisor, foundation program officer or grants manager, consultant or coach, you have a role to play in discovering organizational culture and finding ways to apply what you learn to strengthen nonprofit management strategies.

In this chapter, we share with you a few additional thoughts about *how to use* the ROC process as a complement to other organization development efforts. We also touch briefly on the extreme situation where closing a nonprofit and starting over is a better alternative to discovering and changing organizational culture. In Chapter Five, we conclude with a few recommendations for nonprofit capacity builders about helping leaders make understanding organizational culture a priority.

Throughout our research for the book, we noticed that organizational culture was most visible to organizations at stressful times or times of change that were out of the ordinary. We therefore used this frame of reference in creating the ROC process. High-performing organizations are dealing with the flux and tensions caused by the changing environment almost all the time. Organizational culture can be an important element of management strategies in thriving organizations. By beginning to integrate your understanding of organizational culture into ordinary organization development processes, you can leverage the findings from the ROC process. Common organization development opportunities to utilize organizational culture include ongoing capacity building, strategy development, marketing and image building, theories of change and evaluation, succession planning or post-hire support for a new executive, and restructuring and internal reorganization, to name a few. We discuss these topics in the remainder of this chapter.

Ongoing Capacity Building

If you believe, as we do, that organizational culture lives in every aspect of an organization, then it has a role in responding to everyday management situations. If an organization has never conducted an analysis of its culture, you can apply the entire ROC process to a management challenge. If the organization has already completed an organizational culture summary, you can apply the assessment to the particular challenge, perhaps revisiting the cultural summary using the new challenge as the business objective around which the cultural analysis is resumed.

The following types of organization development issues can be the defining objective that anchors the analysis:

- Creating updated plans to cultivate the right kind of board members
- Updating the board committee structure and committee practices
- Refreshing operational or personnel policies
- Making staff meetings more meaningful and engaging
- Strengthening specific elements of internal organizational communication
- Launching a new department
- Designing a new program

If you are revisiting your organizational culture for the second or third time, you are doing a little "revealing" and a little applying, and you might begin at phase 2, step 2 (Description of the Objective). If some new stressor has popped up, there may be a new aspect of your organizational culture to bring to the surface. You'll be able to do this quickly by spending an hour in a staff meeting at phase 2, step 3 (Share Stories and Create a Mind Map). You do not need to start over or draw a new mind map. Instead, you reflect on whether the new objective you're addressing triggers new stories of survival, new stories of heroes or heroines, or other values you might *add* to your mind map that would be helpful in addressing the new issue. The new stories and additions to your mind map may lead you to updates of your organizational culture summary. Otherwise, if you determine there is no updating to do, you can proceed right to phase 3 to analyze the implications of your organizational culture on the new objective you want to address.

We suspect that once you work on surfacing the hidden truths in your organizational culture two or three times, you'll have a good understanding of its central elements. You can then regularly apply the steps in phase 3 to strengthen management and enhance organizational behavior. Once you've done this a few times, the information about your organizational culture will likely become a routine factor in your management conversations and strategies.

We'll show you how this can work by returning to the Human Rights Institute (HRI) example explored throughout Chapter Three. The objective we worked on in that example was *improving communication between middle managers and senior management to reduce turnover.* In the process of discovering its organizational culture, we identified several core beliefs at HRI that have an impact on communication. In phase 3, we explored how HRI can apply these core beliefs to define actions that will enhance communication between middle and senior managers. (Refer to Exhibit 3.9.) Now let's suppose that six months later, senior management identifies the objective of *increasing public policy advocacy work and decreasing direct service delivery.* HRI can apply the previously identified core beliefs to this management challenge. It would explore how its organizational culture could help achieve the new objective and how this translates into specific action steps. In the example shown in Exhibit 4.1, note that the core beliefs didn't change. What did change is the analysis of the benefits and risks of the core beliefs in terms of their implications for accomplishing the objective. With these steps in place, HRI is positioned to create a new action plan.

Strategy Development

As organizations develop strategies to continue their work, understanding how organizational culture can help or hinder implementation can make the difference between successfully implementing strategic plans and putting the plans on a shelf and wasting the investment.

Exhibit 4.1
How HRI Applies Its Cultural Analysis to a New Objective

HELP	ACTION IMPLICATION
What about our organizational culture will HELP us achieve our objective?	**How could this knowledge help with action planning?**
Belief in small teams and quick decisions	Begin with a small team that has advocacy experience and find something to be successful with quickly.
Belief in hierarchical structure with senior management in charge	Get senior management buy-in early; the leadership position of senior management needs to be valued in the process.
Desire to influence power centers and not risk these relationships	Identify an independent funding source to support advocacy; start with an issue that can be win-win for both HRI and an agency it often works with.
Belief in the importance of the work	Frame actions in terms of how they can positively influence people who are being tortured, persecuted, and displaced, which is a positive motivator for senior management.
Avoidance of conflict	Experiment with different ways of increasing tolerance for conflict and successfully resolving it.

HINDER	ACTION IMPLICATION
What about our organizational culture will HINDER us in achieving this objective?	**How could this knowledge help with action planning?**
Ultimate belief that speed and a small group of leaders making decisions are most effective	Celebrate small successes frequently so that there is evidence of steady progress.
Existing hierarchy and comfort with this structure	Build in a step for senior management to give input and for senior management to be engaged in creating advocacy messages.
Little belief in need for integration and information sharing	Share examples with senior staff about how other organizations coordinate effective advocacy initiatives; work together on a communication strategy that everyone can "try on" together.

In these two examples, consider how understanding organizational culture is increasing the likelihood that these organizations will use their strategic plans.

A community development organization talked a lot in its strategic planning process about the importance of collaboration for its future. However, when the organization stepped back to look at its organizational culture, it discovered that a dominant characteristic was organizational introversion. Although its quiet, steady approach helped it succeed, it really wasn't collaborating with other organizations at the level it thought necessary for future success. As a result, the organization needed to take intentional steps to shift this part of its culture, including developing the confidence of staff to be collaborative.

An organization supporting people with disabilities decided it needed to make new connections in the broader community with audiences outside the disability arena. However, when the board of directors stepped back to look at the organization's culture, members discovered that the nonprofit had few outside connections and some fear of changing a long-held practice of limiting board membership to family members of people with disabilities. The leadership saw that the organization needed to take intentional steps to shift this part of its culture, including changing its by-laws and the way board members were recruited.

Another opportunity to introduce the ROC into strategic planning is during the planning itself when organizations clarify or affirm their "organizational identity" (Drucker, 1999). A discussion about organizational identity is a good time to explore organizational culture for the first time or to revisit the analysis if it has already been conducted. Using organizational culture during strategic planning and during implementation yields important insights to help motivate organization performance.

Marketing and Image Building

At a time when competition for financial support is greater than ever and a growing chorus of voices is questioning how many nonprofit organizations can survive—let alone thrive—in difficult economic times, it is more important than

THE RELATIONSHIP BETWEEN ORGANIZATIONAL CULTURE AND IDENTITY

We consider highlighting organizational identity in the midst of strategic planning to be an example of using organizational culture to enhance performance. Here we look at two approaches which show that organizational identity includes organizational culture elements and demonstrate how organization development practitioners already intuitively use parts of organizational culture to inform the definition of strategic direction for their clients.

Before Paige Teegarden established Think Outside, she and Denice Hinden worked together for more than six years at Managance Consulting & Coaching. During that time, they helped clients explore their organizational identity as part of strategic planning. The elements in their organizational identity statements drew in part on the work of Drucker (1999) and offer an example of including organizational culture in a key part of strategic planning. Their organizational identity statements included the following:

- Mission—defined as the difference an organization aims to make in the "world" (Drucker, 2008) (Note: "World" is a term of art here. Each organization defines its own boundaries.)

- Vision—how the organization imagines the world will actually look when the organization accomplishes its mission

- Core operating values—how the organization wants its customers to experience the organization

- Theory of action—beliefs that frame the unique way the organization does its work

- Customers—the people whom the organization exists to serve (its primary customers) and those who help the organization be successful (its supporting customers)

- Business model—how the organization raises funds, earns income, or both

- Organizational culture—the deep underlying assumptions that help and hinder an organization in implementing strategies to accomplish its mission. Paige and Denice made organizational culture a named part of the identity discussions during the research for this book.

In his recent book *The Nonprofit Strategic Revolution* (2008), David LaPiana also discusses the importance of having a clear organizational identity that articulates an organization's understanding of its market and competitive advantage. In his examples, an organization's leaders address the following identity questions to the organization, using the business model to answer them:

- Who are you? (What are your mission and vision?)
- What work do you do? (What are the activities you undertake to advance your mission and achieve your vision?) This is also called scope of work.
- How do you do your work? (What are the structures, operations, budgets, policies, and procedures that support your activities, and how do you attract and use financial resources?)
- How do you maintain adequate and consistent finances?

LaPiana emphasizes how understanding identity helps the organization identify and respond quickly to opportunities and challenges. Although his identity questions don't explicitly include organizational culture, the answers to his questions will contain hints about it.

ever for nonprofits to be clear about how their organizational culture shapes their programs, services, and contributions to the public good. This is important, in part, because it will help distinguish nonprofits from one another. Moreover, as new forms of social networking and digital media expand and create more outlets for nonprofits to tell the story of their good work, understanding organizational culture can be a useful tool for crafting compelling messages that reach and stick with intended audiences.

In his book *Branding for Success!* Larry Checco explains that "branding represents a short cut, an instant recognition of what an organization stands for." He goes on to explain further that "it is the overall image or impression people have of your work, your reputation, your staff, your leadership, your organization's culture and core values, as well as its programs, services and products" (2005, p. 21). By understanding organizational culture more deeply, your organization can creatively integrate elements of it into your marketing material and messages in a way that is unique to your approach and mission (p. 21).

After your organization implements the ROC and has a solid sense of the key elements in its organizational culture, you may find it helpful to explore the archetypal images around which to create or enhance the unique brand identity of your organization. Mark and Pearson's *The Hero and the Outlaw: Building Extraordinary Brands Through the Power of Archetypes* (2001) offers a fascinating and in-depth exploration of this topic.

Applying a Theory of Change and Program Evaluation

Evaluating organization or program outcomes and impact is an especially ripe opportunity for surfacing the deep underlying assumptions in an organization's culture. There are two parts of a program evaluation system where understanding organizational culture can be especially helpful. One is in the creation or examination of the theory of change or program logic model. The other is in using program evaluation findings to strengthen programs and services.

A theory of change or logic model expresses why an organization believes its service delivery approach will accomplish its desired results and mission. The theory or logic lays out the rationale (the beliefs and values) of the approach. At the root of a theory of change are the beliefs or values an organization holds about how change is likely to happen in the world. These beliefs or values are then visible in the way the organization structures it programs and creates rules or guidelines for how the programs or services are implemented. Understanding the deep underlying assumptions in your organizational culture can inform the rationale—the underlying theory of the organization's work. (For more information on logic models, see Mattessich, 2003.)

Let's return to the example of the organization supporting people with disabilities that wanted to make new connections in the broader community with audiences outside the disability arena. This organization also has deeply held beliefs that every person, regardless of developmental disability, has the right to choose the kind of life he or she wants to live in the least restrictive environment possible; that natural and voluntary supports are essential ingredients in authentic acceptance in any community; and that true inclusion in communities occurs when individuals with developmental disabilities are empowered to make their own decisions and are welcomed into and supported by the communities where they choose to live. These beliefs in turn inform the organization's logic model and the way all staff members are expected to do their jobs. By discovering the elements of organizational culture that are implied in its logic model, the organization could use this information in training new staff, figuring out ways to strengthen its approach, or changing parts of the model that may not be working well.

Once an organization has completed a program evaluation, it usually has new information to use to enhance service delivery. This means the program has to make changes, which staff or other stakeholders may resist. By thinking about how elements of organizational culture can help or hinder that change, the organization may be more successful in effectively responding to evaluation findings.

Succession Planning, Transition Planning, or Settling In Post-Hire

In Chapter Two, we shared with you a few examples of organizations that were in the post-hiring phase of a leadership transition, where the new executive director was struggling in some way to work within or shift the organizational culture. In the early 2000s, with support from the Annie E. Casey Foundation, a national collaboration of capacity builders conducted research and developed the Executive Transition Management (ETM) framework to help nonprofits prepare for the anticipated wave of founder and long-term executive director transitions through 2020.[1]

Through this research and subsequent work in managing many leadership transitions, we have learned that three key times for surfacing organizational culture are (1) the first six months after a new executive director is hired (post-hire period), (2) during emergency succession planning, and (3) when the organization is planning for a leadership transition. In the post-hire period when a new executive is just learning the lay of the land, the ROC can be used to surface elements of organizational culture the new executive can then use in thinking about his or her own leadership behavior, new practices to introduce, and existing practices that he or she might want to change.

Emergency succession planning is a way for boards and executives to be prepared for unplanned leadership transition. The opportunity to be prepared removes the emotion that often arises when a transition comes up in an emergency or when there are other surprises. The ROC can be a step in emergency succession planning; its results can be used to inform what the organization includes in its emergency succession plan document in the event of a leadership change.

In the event that an organization does not have an emergency succession plan and is faced with a leadership transition, an early step in the ETM framework is for the board of directors to take stock of the organization's circumstances and its sense of direction to provide context for deciding what kind of leadership it needs. It is in this space of strategic visioning that discovering or applying understanding about organizational culture can be very helpful, both in identifying the attributes and competencies important to seek out in a future leader and in assisting candidates for the job in understanding what may be required of them to be successful in the organization.

Restructuring

Internal reorganization, merging, starting up a new organization, and making a decision to close are all times in the life of an organization when discovering and understanding elements of organizational culture can be invaluable.

Internal Reorganization   Internal reorganization is a time when work flow, long-term habits, practices, and procedures are affected by the realigning of job responsibilities and how parts of an organization or department relate to each other. We have experience indicating that well-designed strategies and good new structure decisions are more likely to emerge when the organization is equipped with an understanding of its culture.

Merger   Other authors have identified understand organizational culture as an important component in the process of bringing two or more different organizations together in a merger (LaPiana, 2000; LaPiana et al., 2004; McLaughlin, 1998). LaPiana and his colleagues point out that "Corporate culture causes people from different organizations to have subtle differences in their perceptions. In the normal course of business that is usually not an issue, since visitors to an organization know they are visitors. However, during merger negotiations, participants tend to forget this fact, to bring their own corporate culture to the negotiating table, and to expect others to share their understanding of things (2004, p. 72).

LaPiana et al. explain further that once two or more organizations make a decision to merge, the board "integration committee" must provide leadership in fostering a culture where board members think in "us" terms—as opposed to "us and them"—and it has to take on the practical task of putting the new board in place (2004, p. 73). Just as important is paying attention to organizational culture at the programmatic level. LaPiana et al. remind us that "careful attention to cultural integration within programs is critical to the overall integration process. An inability to blend cultures of the merging organizations makes it difficult, if not impossible, to effectively merge the organizations into a smoothly operating entity" (p. 111). The ROC could easily be included in the course of merger discussions, first by each organization in the process of deciding if a merger makes sense, and then together in creating an integrated organizational culture that reflects the views and interests of all parties.

Start-Up   Whereas merging organizations have to consider how to blend existing organizational cultures, leaders starting up a new organization have a "blank sheet of paper" when it comes to organizational culture. In this situation, the organization founders could use the ROC process as an outline for envisioning the kind of culture they'd like to create and what management strategies might support the vision. In this way, an understanding of organizational culture can become an integral part of the organization from its inception.

Shutdown   A final consideration in organization restructuring is the option of closing. Although there are many circumstances that give rise to a decision to close an organization, we are talking here about the extreme cases where the organizational culture may be too toxic and would be too costly to try to fix. In these cases, financial viability may also be a factor, but it is not the central one. Closing the organization and beginning again with a different board, different leadership, and different staff with fresh ideas and a fresh commitment to the particular mission may be the best option. Here, closing an organization is a management strategy for managing change in a particular type of organizational culture. If a subsequent decision is made to start up a new organization, the "blank sheet" (start-up) notion would apply.

Nonprofit organizations are started and closed every day. Although not always an easy turn of events, this is part of the natural cycle of organizational life that creates the opportunity to bring fresh perspective to our communities.

As leaders and capacity builders of nonprofit organizations, we must be committed to creating and sustaining organizational environments that staff and volunteers are excited to be part of and that motivate them to do their best work. If, from time to time, we come across a nonprofit organization where it is nearly impossible to determine the investment required to achieve this kind of organizational culture or unclear whether the investment would achieve the desired outcome, then closing and beginning again may make sense. Nonprofit organizations do not have the luxury of risking precious resources on outcomes not likely to be realized.

Denver Options in Colorado is an example of an organization created when starting over seemed to be the best choice. Since 1991, Denver Options has been responsible for coordinating the state's services for people with intellectual and developmental disabilities. Prior to the creation of Denver Options, another organization had the responsibility. Stephen Block had been hired as its fifth executive director in six years. He found an organization where, as he described it, "The culture was in disarray. There was a lack of trust. People paid attention to themselves to protect their own interests instead of focusing on the people needing support from the organization. There was also dysfunction on the board as members focused on their own interests in the contract with the state and not on the organization itself." Given his nonprofit management background, Block believed that when an organization like this fails to perform, it should lose the contract and be closed. Otherwise it would have taken several years to fix. The State of Colorado followed his recommendation and issued a Request For Proposal for a new organization. Stephen responded with the concept of Denver Options.

A notable part of the creation story of Denver Options is how the organizational culture was framed. Block was not deeply familiar with the industry of disability services, but he was steeped in nonprofit management. He explained that when Denver Options was created, he invited twenty-five people—new board members and new staff—to spend the day at a botanical garden with a facilitator to explore their hopes for future, what the community needed, and the type of organization and values they wanted. (This was similar to the outdoor experience described at the end of Chapter Three.) The themes of the day formed the mission, values, and beliefs that still serve the organization today.

In our interview, Block explained that an organization's leader plays an important role as a keeper of the organizational culture. He, along with the senior staff, is intentional about keeping the values and beliefs in the organizational culture present to everyone connected to the organization's work.

In this chapter we've touched on some of the key opportunities we see for organizational capacity builders—staff and consultants—to apply this new understanding about organizational culture to organization development. In Chapter Five we offer some final thoughts about ways to make the process a valuable and enlightening experience.

Recommendations for Nonprofit Leaders and Capacity Builders

From the beginning of our journey to understand what organizational culture means in the nonprofit sector, we've focused on what would be helpful to the various audiences for the book—nonprofit staff, board members, consultants, coaches, facilitators, trainers, philanthropists, educators, and other stakeholders. This chapter is for any nonprofit leader or capacity builder who has a primary concern about organizational capacity and effectiveness. It is written assuming that you are an "outsider" to the organization. We suggest a variety of actions to make organizational culture an integral part of your work, and we offer several suggestions about how to engage organization stakeholders in this conversation. In our experience, developing a mind shift about organizational culture and using it to your benefit takes practice; it must become a new habit. We close the chapter with a few ideas for further research. We hope that others with interest in this topic will help us pursue additional evidenced-based studies that will take our collective understanding about organizational culture to new levels.

FOUR PRACTICES FOR CONSIDERATION

Although you will of course approach your work from the perspective of your particular field and position, we urge you to integrate the following four practices into your organization development work.

Be mindful of organizational culture elements that lie beneath the surface.
For example, you might begin an organizational culture mind map as part of
the learning process with your clients and deepen the information you routinely
gather. Learn about the organization's creation story and the community or
societal environment at the time of its founding. Learn about its survival stories
and hero and heroine stories. Listen for spoken and unspoken assumptions that
provide a rationale for organizational behaviors that are not included in written mission statements and core values statements, public pronouncements and
platitudes, annual reports, Web sites, or even the rhetoric in funding proposals. These constitute only the tip of the iceberg (see Figure 5.1). Remember that
organizational culture lives in the walk, not the talk.

**Be intentional about creating opportunities for organization leaders to
experience the value of discovering and understanding organizational culture.** For example, find some element of the organization's culture that demonstrates the link between the underlying assumptions and organizational
behavior. It could be a positive element to be reinforced or a problem element
to think about shifting. Discuss the element and brainstorm a few ways to take
action. Reflect on the outcome of the action and its value. Finish by supporting
the organization leader in making these steps an integral part of management
practices.

One way to help leaders accomplish this is through executive or group coaching that offers support for trying out and reflecting on their experience with
new approaches. For example, when the size of an organization's staff increased
beyond what the executive director could directly supervise herself, her coach
helped her find a comfortable way to delegate some of this responsibility. This
was particularly difficult because a deep assumption in this organization's culture was that everyone had equal access to leadership. With the help of a coach,
the executive director guided all staff in the development of a new organizational
structure and implementation strategy that staff were prepared to adopt because
they had helped create it.

**Be courageous in speaking out when you believe elements of organizational
culture or its artifacts need to change in some way.** Often leaders cannot see
their own circumstances objectively, and not all leaders have the ability to easily
move from Heifetz and Linsky's metaphorical dance floor up to the balcony to
see the big organizational picture (2002). The greatest value of a nonprofit capacity builder is in being an informed, objective voice that can offer constructive

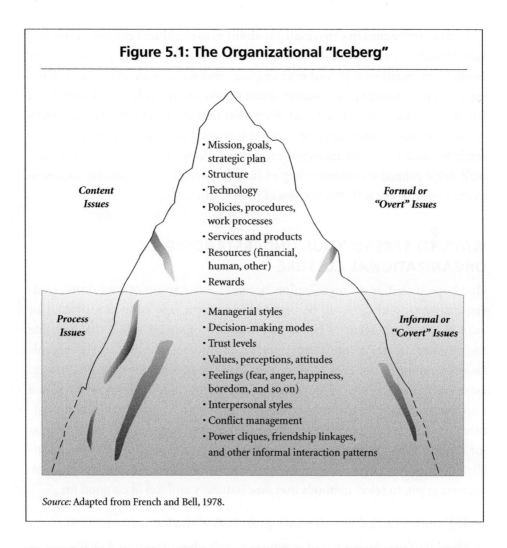

Figure 5.1: The Organizational "Iceberg"

Content Issues

- Mission, goals, strategic plan
- Structure
- Technology
- Policies, procedures, work processes
- Services and products
- Resources (financial, human, other)
- Rewards

Formal or "Overt" Issues

Process Issues

- Managerial styles
- Decision-making modes
- Trust levels
- Values, perceptions, attitudes
- Feelings (fear, anger, happiness, boredom, and so on)
- Interpersonal styles
- Conflict management
- Power cliques, friendship linkages, and other informal interaction patterns

Informal or "Covert" Issues

Source: Adapted from French and Bell, 1978.

ideas to help nonprofits be the best organizations they can be. If we are going to be in the business of creating strong organizations, then we have to be willing to be honest and open about where change is really needed. For example, for four years an organization's staff had told management that a change was needed in its approach to quarterly staff meetings, but the request always fell on deaf ears. Finally, the organization development consultant took on the discussion because it simply had to happen. This was done in a supportive way in the context of an understanding on the part of management of how the organization was evolving and how it could change long-held traditions that were integral elements in its culture.

Engage colleagues in conversations about organizational culture. As professionals with the best interests of the whole nonprofit sector in mind, capacity builders are positioned to lead organization- and sector-wide dialogue employing accurate language and concepts about organizational culture. We encourage you to integrate our research and discussion into electronic discussion groups or forums, community dialogues, special interest groups, continuing education seminars, and nonprofit management courses. As we all use this information, we'll build collective understanding of how important organizational culture is to the performance and effectiveness of nonprofits.

WAYS TO SPREAD YOUR UNDERSTANDING OF ORGANIZATIONAL CULTURE

Our hope is that as an organization becomes more aware of its culture, leaders, managers, and staff will be better able to form new cultural artifacts (for example, new management behaviors) and new espoused values that mitigate the negative aspects of the culture and build on its assets. But just as organizational culture is not easy to shift, new management habits are not simple to establish. Consequently, we hope many of you reading this book will become champions of the idea that a deep and rich understanding of organizational culture can yield invaluable insight into organizational behavior and build context for making strategic choices. There are many ways organizations can intentionally integrate awareness of organizational culture into their day-to-day work. We encourage you to select methods that flow naturally and feel like a good fit:

- Tell "culture stories" at staff meetings and talk about lessons from the stories.
- Schedule time during board meetings to talk about assets and challenges in the organizational culture.
- Periodically reflect on how organizational culture is affecting decisions.
- Rotate staff responsibility for being the "conscience" of the organizational culture in strategy discussions. You might also include this responsibility in the position description for one or more staff members.

As you experiment and find effective methods for using organizational culture information, we hope you will share it with us and fellow champions of this work. Please visit www.revealorganizationalculture.com.

AN AGENDA FOR FUTURE RESEARCH

Our journey through the literature and experiences of organizational culture has already been a long one, but it is just beginning. In many ways, this book raises almost as many questions as it answers. We sincerely hope that it raises new questions for you as well. Here are just a few of the questions we identified for possible future research:

- Do boards of directors have a different culture from that of the organizations they govern? If so, what does this mean for organization leadership and management?

- What new perspective would we gain if we looked at organizational culture through the different lenses of client or customer needs, diversity, political theory, civic engagement or participation theory, flexibility and innovation theory, or failure theory?

- Can new leaders with different values from those of previous leadership significantly change an organization's culture?

- What can organizational culture tell us in environments where the values of leadership and staff members are in conflict?

- Can an organization's culture or its artifacts be changed if leadership resists efforts to do so? If so, how does a change agent proceed? What skills do change agents need to facilitate this kind of change?

- What role do external stakeholders play in affecting an organization's culture? How does the influence of founding leaders on the formation of organizational culture compare in nonprofit organizations and for-profit businesses?

- Is there a qualitative difference in the management competency of nonprofit organizations that discover elements of their organizational culture and routinely apply what they learn in their organizations, as compared to organizations that choose not to do this?

From our perspective, the most important question for future research is whether or not a deeper understanding of organizational culture in fact helps leaders of nonprofit organizations effectively navigate through stressful times or periods of change. In our research for this book, we did not have the opportunity to see the "end of the story." We laid the groundwork for this question to be answered, perhaps in our own future work or through the work of others.

IN CLOSING

It is our hope that what we have learned thus far and shared in this book will help move organizational culture into the forefront of conversations about how to strengthen the effectiveness and impact of nonprofit organizations. Because virtually all the research and publications examining organizational culture to date have focused on the private sector—particularly large corporations—this is an area where the nonprofit sector has tremendous potential for new learning and growth.

The late Peter Drucker predicted before his death that similar to the ways in which business was the most important factor in the nineteenth century and government the most important factor in the twentieth century, the social sector (Drucker's term for the nonprofit sector) would be the most important factor in the twenty-first century (Hesselbein, 2001). With the increasing importance of the sector throughout the world, nonprofit leaders and capacity builders need new tools and resources. We believe that the ability to more deeply understand organizational culture and the myriad of ways it manifests itself provides a rich backdrop of knowledge not yet revealed and used to its fullest potential. When understood and routinely used by nonprofit leaders and capacity builders, this knowledge will ultimately enhance the quality of life for all of us. In our judgment, the stakes are too high to settle for anything less.

W̲e are indebted to each of the following thought leaders and capacity builders for their time and thoughts. We interviewed each of them to help inform our thinking about nonprofits and organizational culture.

Heather Berthoud of Berthoud Consulting, Washington, DC, has been providing organization development support to organizations for more than twenty years. She helps people realize the benefits of working effectively with differences and creating unifying visions, plans, and processes. Prior to her work as a consultant, she was responsible for training design and delivery for the National Abortion Rights Action League and its local network. In addition to her consulting practice, she is faculty for the American University/NTL Institute. She has a BS in biology from the University of Pennsylvania and an MS in organization development from American University/NTL Institute.

Stephen Block is the director of the Nonprofit Management Program at the University of Colorado Denver's School of Public Affairs (SPA). He earned his MSW from Indiana University and PhD from SPA. As a Fulbright Scholar, he taught at Moscow State University of Management and is currently involved in activities to advance nongovernmental organization (NGO) management education in Russia. His teaching and research interests include nonprofit boards of directors, executive leadership, and nonprofit organizational behavior and development. Block has written numerous journal articles and books, including *Why Nonprofits Fail: Overcoming Founder's Syndrome, Fundphobia, and*

Other Obstacles to Success (Jossey-Bass, 2004), and *Perfect Nonprofit Boards: Myths, Paradoxes and Paradigms* (Simon & Schuster, 1998). His latest nonprofit management textbook is in the Russian language for use in universities and NGOs throughout Russia. Block was also the founding executive director of Denver Options, Denver, Colorado.

Peter Brinckerhoff is an internationally renowned trainer, author, and consultant to nonprofit organizations. He brings years of experience in the field to his work, as he is a former board member of local, state, and national nonprofits, and has worked on the staff and as executive director of two regional nonprofits. Since founding his consulting firm, Corporate Alternatives, in 1982, Brinckerhoff has helped thousands of organizations become more "mission-capable" (effective in implementing their missions). He is the award-winning author of the highly acclaimed books *Mission-Based Management* (Second and Third Editions), *Mission-Based Management Workbook, Financial Empowerment, Mission-Based Marketing* (Second Edition) and its associated *Mission-Based Marketing Workbook, Faith-Based Management,* and *Social Entrepreneurship*, all published by Wiley, and *Nonprofit Stewardship*, published by Fieldstone Alliance. Brinckerhoff's book, *Generations: The Challenge of a Lifetime for Your Nonprofit*, was published by Fieldstone Alliance in March 2007, and was awarded the Terry McAdam award for best nonprofit book by the Alliance for Nonprofit Management. It was the third time Brinckerhoff has won this prestigious award.

Robert Hoffman of Robert Hoffman & Associates, Columbia, MD, has been a human resource development consultant for over thirty-five years. His capacity to connect with his clients of all ages and experiences grows from the fun and humor he cultivated as a fifth- and sixth-grade teacher at the beginning of his career. In the 1960s, Hoffman was a director of a community action agency. In the 1970s, he was an elected local official in his New Jersey community. In recent years, Hoffman's primary interest has been in developing urban and rural youth for leadership in their communities. To this end, he is founder of a nonprofit conference and leadership retreat center in West Virginia. Hoffman has a master's degree in personnel and guidance from Montclair State University and additional course work in gestalt psychology, large-scale systems change, and appreciative inquiry.

Dr. Paul C. Light is NYU Wagner's Paulette Goddard Professor of Public Service and founding principal investigator of the Organizational Performance Initiative. Until joining NYU, Light served as the Douglas Dillon Senior Fellow at the Brookings Institution, founding director of its Center for Public Service, and vice president and director of the Governmental Studies Program. He has served previously as director of the Public Policy Program at the Pew Charitable Trusts and associate dean and professor of public affairs at the University of Minnesota's Hubert Humphrey Institute of Public Affairs.

Light has written eighteen books, including the award-winning *Thickening Government* (Brookings Institution) and *The Tides of Reform* (Yale University Press). He is also a coauthor of a best-selling American government textbook, *Government by the People* (Prentice Hall). His research interests include bureaucracy, civil service, Congress, entitlement programs, the executive branch, government reform, nonprofit effectiveness, organizational change, and the political appointment process.

Carol Lukas is former president of Fieldstone Alliance and former director of national services for the Amherst H. Wilder Foundation. She has been executive director of nonprofit organizations, a trustee of a community foundation, a consultant in a Fortune 500 company, and a small business owner. She has more than twenty-five years of consulting and training experience with nonprofits, government, foundations, businesses, and collaboratives. Lukas focuses on building the capacity of national networks and organizations and on strengthening connections between the public, private, and nonprofit sectors as they address urban issues. She specializes in helping organizations and collaboratives plan and manage change in strategic direction and organizational structure and capacity. She is author and coauthor of *Consulting with Nonprofits: A Practitioner's Guide* (Fieldstone Alliance), *Strengthening Nonprofit Performance: A Funder's Guide to Capacity Building* (Fieldstone

Alliance), and *The Wilder Nonprofit Field Guide to Conducting Community Forums* (Wilder Press).

Ruth McCambridge has more than thirty-five years of experience working in and with social justice and community-based nonprofits. For twenty of these years, McCambridge worked in and managed community-based and social change organizations. In 1987, she took a long-standing interest in organizational dynamics to the Boston Foundation, where she developed a statewide management assistance program for homeless and battered women's shelters and managed the Fund for the Homeless. She stayed at the Boston Foundation for ten years, helping along the way to launch and manage a number of other collaboratively funded capacity-building initiatives.

McCambridge is now the editor in chief of the *Nonprofit Quarterly*, an innovative journal for nonprofit leaders. She considers herself, at base, an organizer; her work is motivated by a deep belief in the need for organizations that help people with relatively little influence to develop their individual and collective voice and power.

Richard L. Moyers is director of programs at the Meyer Foundation, which includes a management assistance program for grantees, support for broad efforts to strengthen the nonprofit sector, and a cash flow loan program. Prior to joining the Meyer Foundation in November 2003, Rick was executive director of the Ohio Association of Nonprofit Organizations (OANO), a statewide coalition of more than 650 nonprofits that provides leadership, education, and advocacy to strengthen Ohio's nonprofit sector. Before joining OANO in 1999, Rick spent seven years at BoardSource, concluding his tenure as vice president for programs and services.

Moyers currently serves on the boards of Imagination Stage and the Washington Regional Association of Grantmakers. He is a frequent speaker and trainer on nonprofit management and leadership issues, and has written for *The Chronicle of Philanthropy* and *Nonprofit Times*. He is the author of *The Nonprofit Chief Executive's Ten Basic Responsibilities* (BoardSource, 2006), and was the coauthor of *Daring to Lead 2006*, the report on a national survey of executive directors conducted in partnership with CompassPoint Nonprofit Services.

Dr. David Renz is the Beth K. Smith/Missouri Chair in Nonprofit Leadership and the director of the Midwest Center for Nonprofit Leadership at the University of Missouri-Kansas City. Renz teaches and conducts research on nonprofit and public service leadership and governance, and he helps organizations develop programs to strengthen quality, innovation, and effectiveness. Much of Renz's work focuses on helping organizations and communities design and successfully implement major change and development initiatives. During his career, Renz has served in several senior executive positions in state and regional government. He served for five years as the executive director of the Metropolitan Council of the Twin Cities, and spent six years serving as assistant commissioner for administration for the State of Minnesota Department of Labor and Industry. Renz's career experience also includes major research and development projects for foundation, university, government, and private sector sponsors. Renz has worked with and for nonprofit and public service organizations in many capacities. In addition to his extensive consulting work, he has served on several state government advisory councils and groups and as an officer and board member for nonprofits and voluntary associations, including service on boards and advisory committees at the local, regional, and national levels.

PERSPECTIVES ON ORGANIZATIONAL CULTURE

All these thought leaders and capacity builders had similar definitions of organizational culture, offering some version of the following: organizational culture is a set of shared beliefs, values, assumptions, and norms. Several informants provided additional comments that are useful when trying to understand a particular nonprofit organization's culture.

First, highlighting *behavior*, both Carol Lukas and Peter Brinckerhoff emphasized that organizational culture is revealed in the behavior of organizations and not necessarily the spoken or written statements. Brinckerhoff put it this way: "Talk without behavior is not culture." Lukas explained, "Behavior is the most important measure of culture; behavior is the manifestation of culture."

Second, McCambridge suggested that we need to pay particular attention to the *stories and language* that people in nonprofits are using. She said, "Since organizations are human systems, they are impacted by the way we humans conceptualize things—our paradigms, symbols, and stories." She also talked about the importance of "carefully listening to the language that people are using, and thinking about what that may indicate about the organization's culture." We know that language and stories can tell us a lot about the meaning that people are attaching to events. For example, imagine an organization that is going through a challenging time, and it deals with it by convening groups of staff and stakeholders for a discussion of strategy and opportunities; now imagine what hints it would give you about the organizational culture if those convenings were called "war councils" or "listening sessions." What if the challenge itself were talked about in terms of conflict, and staff made such statements as "I can't believe they would hurt us this way" or "We need to protect ourselves, find shelter so that we can find our voice."

An example of stories from McCambridge includes one about the success stories from domestic violence shelters. She says, "Their success stories were about individual successes, about 'saving' women from violence, and the staff that were successful in these organizations tended to be empathetic, very sensitive, and motivated to 'save women.'" Notice that "saving women" suggests a crisis, a do-or-die situation. Further, the successful staff placed a lot of value and faith in being sensitive to the needs of the women. When you listen to stories about the heroic nature of battered women who got away from their abusers and the facilitative counselor who encouraged her along the way, you collect wonderful information to cull through as you try to uncover organizational culture.

Third, Heather Berthoud and Bob Hoffman, longtime capacity builders, mentioned using the *appreciative inquiry approach*. The idea here is to take something familiar to many nonprofit capacity builders—asking probing questions about what is working—and applying that to the topic of organizational culture. Berthoud notes, "From appreciative inquiry we have the opportunity to value the parts of the deep culture that support delivering on the mission." The framework of appreciative inquiry would certainly appear to offer a good mind-set for revealing organizational culture. Similarly, David Renz used Warren Bennis's concept of "management of meaning" as a guide for helping staff deal with a significant change in behaviors that were butting up against cultural assumptions. In this model, Renz directly asked staff about what they thought their behaviors meant in response to the requested changes and what their concerns were.

Finally, Rick Moyer talked about the importance of *founders and long-term executives* in building the organization's culture. He gave examples of the expectations that founders and long-term executives set, ranging from whether meetings start on time and whether people take notes to who they hire. Moyer and Brinckerhoff also spoke more generally about leadership. Moyer said, "Over time, unless they make conscious effort to do it differently, leaders hire people who think and value the same things they do." Brinckerhoff said, "If leadership models behavior, it becomes part of the culture." Thus looking explicitly at founders or longtime executives can give hints about the organization's culture today.

Our informants were also helpful in highlighting two common beliefs about nonprofits and their cultures: (1) organizational cultures are closely bound to the organization's clients and their issues or problems, and (2) organizational culture is heavily influenced by the culture of the broader field of work or mission in which the nonprofit is involved. Although these ideas are somewhat related, we'll talk about them separately to better understand them.

Both Lukas and McCambridge point out that in some cases nonprofits begin to take on elements of the client's dysfunctional behaviors. For example, Lukas noted that she has seen organizations serving battered women, crime victims, and people who live in poverty take on a "victim" mentality, which isn't helpful to the organization's mission. The victim mentality might reflect the following kinds of beliefs: "Those in power are always out to get us," or "We need to be strong and stand up to them, but we are weak, we can't do that," or "We're too small to impact that." If an organization acts on these kinds of beliefs it will have difficulty forming strong partnerships with other agencies, it will have difficulty making bold decisions, and it may even lash out at those who could otherwise help it, such as strong and successful businesses.

Several of our informants pointed out a connection between the need or issue that the nonprofit is set up to deal with and elements of the organization's culture. In one example, Moyers talked about a conflict resolution organization that was fraught with conflict and even set up structures to promote conflict. Its bylaws called for every seat on the board to be contested—with at least two people running for each open position. It appears that the board's belief in the role of conflict in everyday life and their knowledge about conflict became assumptions about the correct way to come to truth or agreement in all situations, even internal ones.

Berthoud offered the example of a labor union. Labor unions are fundamentally organizations that strive to equalize the strength between management and employees. They play the roles of "go-between," "strong negotiator," and "fighter."

Berthoud described the "political intrigue" within a labor union where she worked. There was significant emphasis on the political, on the campaign, and on conflict as opposed to direct engagement. Conversations were about "what she must have meant" or "war strategy." The broader purpose of labor unions, to be a power equalizer and strong fighter, seemed to have become the main narrative of the organization itself and the way it dealt with its own internal issues. Union leadership believed that power analysis was the right way to view labor-management relations and the right way to address internal conflicts.

In these two examples, our informants show us ways that underlying beliefs and values that have worked well for the organization in dealing with its external world become the assumed way to manage the inner workings of the organization. These examples suggest cautions about some of the ways organizational culture can challenge managers and leaders of nonprofits.

Our interviews with thought leaders and capacity builders were in line with much of what we read in the general literature, and they pointed out some important elements about nonprofits and organizational culture. Specifically, they said,

- Pay close attention to behavior, not just what is written or what leadership says

- Use stories and language as a source of information to analyze when thinking about organizational culture

- Consider the potential of appreciative inquiry as a mind-set and method for assessing organizational culture

- Acknowledge the critical nature of founders and long-term leaders in setting culture

- Look for interaction between the need, client, or field that the nonprofit operates in and the organizational culture

There are many "tools" on the market that promise to help you assess or measure your organization's culture. In our early research for this book, we identified about a dozen existing tools that claim to assess or profile organizational culture. We ultimately chose to review three approaches: the qualitative approach, developed by Edgar Schein; the Denison Organizational Culture Survey, developed by Daniel Denison; and the KenXa™ Cultural Insight (KCI), created by Carol Pearson. We chose these three tools for several reasons. First, they were developed through extensive research and have different clearly articulated theoretical underpinnings. Second, they are popular and may be applicable to nonprofit organizations. Third, they are exemplary of the available approaches to understanding organizational culture. (Among them, Schein's work is the most often referenced.) Finally, we had some access to the scholars who designed the tools. We ultimately used what we learned from these tools in developing our own Revealing Organizational Culture (ROC) process introduced in this book.

SCHEIN'S PROCESS FOR UNDERSTANDING AND CHANGING ORGANIZATIONAL CULTURE

In *The Corporate Culture Survival Guide*, Schein (1999) outlined a six-step process for understanding an organization's culture and determining whether it will help or hinder the leaders' goals. The final step helps members in the organization determine how to change an element of the culture. The process relies on group discussion and reflection. The six steps are as follows:

Step 1: State a business problem and clarify definitions

Step 2: Describe what really happens in the organization

Step 3: State espoused values

Step 4: Compare values and artifacts to uncover tacit assumptions

Step 5: Determine whether assumptions will help or hinder change

Step 6: Change an element of culture

For more information, see *The Corporate Culture Survival Guide.*

DENISON ORGANIZATIONAL CULTURE SURVEY (DOCS)

The Denison Organizational Culture Survey is a sixty-item survey developed by Daniel R. Denison and William S. Neale, MA, MILR, that measures the specific aspects of an organization's culture based on the four traits and twelve management practices of the Denison Model. All employees are invited to complete the assessment. Participants answer five questions on twelve indices that cover each element of the model. For example, the five questions about empowerment cover how employees are involved in their work, the level in the organization where decisions are made, how information is widely shared, how people feel about the impact they can have on the organization, and the extent of business planning in the organization and their involvement in it. The answers are on a scale of 1 to 5 (plus a "not applicable" option). Individual surveys are collectively tabulated into a graphical profile that compares the organization's culture to a global normative database of more than seven hundred higher- and lower-performing organizations. For more information, see www.denisonculture.com.

KENXA CULTURAL INDICATOR SURVEY (KCI)

The KCI is administered through a questionnaire that organization employees or members of the participating group are invited to complete within a defined period of time. The indicator instrument is most effective in its online Web-based format, which allows for the most comprehensive analysis of the data. The KCI helps organizations identify predominant archetypes in each of four critical subsystems in organizations. The four subsystems, which are based on Maslow's hierarchy of needs, are Material/Safety, Human Community/Belonging, Production/Self-Esteem, and Learning/Self-Actualization. By helping organizations identify the predominant archetype in each subsystem, the KCI helps organizations better understand their tendencies or preferences. It must be managed by a qualified administrator, typically an organization development consultant, strategic planning consultant, or human resource director, who has completed training in use of the instrument. For more information, see www.capt.org and www.herowithin.com.

ADDITIONAL TOOLS

The following are other tools you may find useful:

- Shifting the Organization's Culture: A Self-Assessment Guide, found at www.trafford.com
- Cultural Compass, found at www.CommunicationIdeas.com
- *Diagnosing Organizational Culture*, a book and instrument by Roger Harrison and Herb Stokes, which can be found at http://www.pfeiffer.com/WileyCDA/
- "An Organizational Culture Assessment Using the Competing Values Framework: A Profile of Ohio State University Extension," a paper by Angel A. Berrio, which is found in *Journal of Extension*, April 2003, and at www.joe.org/joe/2003april/a3.shtml
- Organizational Culture Inventory, by Human Synergistics, Inc., found at www.humansynergistics.com
- Organizational Culture Profile (OCP), by C. A. Reilly, J. Chatman, and D. E. Caldwell, found at www.uwec.edu/Sampsow/Measures/CultureOCP.htm
- Pearson Marr Archetype Indicator (PMAI), found at www.capt.org

APPENDIX C   ABOUT MIND MAPS AND MIND MAPPING

What is a mind map? A mind map is a powerful graphic technique that provides a universal key to unlock the potential of the brain. It harnesses the full range of cortical skills—word, image, number, logic, rhythm, color, and spatial awareness—in a single, uniquely powerful manner. In so doing, it gives you the freedom to roam the infinite expanses of your brain. The mind map can be applied to every aspect of life where improved learning and clearer thinking will enhance human performance.

What do you need to make a mind map? Because mind maps are so easy to create and so natural, the ingredients for your "mind map recipe" are very few:

- Blank unlined paper
- Colored pens and pencils
- Your brain
- Your imagination

Steps to Making a Mind Map

1. Start in the *center* of a blank page turned sideways. Why? Because starting in the center gives your brain freedom to spread out in all directions and to express itself more freely and naturally.

2. Use an *image* or *picture* for your central idea. Why? Because an image is worth a thousand words and helps you use your imagination. A central

Mind Map excerpt made using ThinkBuzan's iMindMap, from www.ThinkBuzan.com

image is more interesting, keeps you focused, helps you concentrate, and gives your brain more of a buzz!

3. Use *colors* throughout. Why? Because colors are as exciting to your brain as images are. Color adds extra vibrancy and life to your mind map, adds tremendous energy to your creative thinking, and is fun!

4. *Connect* your main branches to the central image and connect your second- and third-level branches to the first and second levels, and so on. Why? Because your brain works by association. It likes to link two (or three or four) things together. If you connect the branches, you will understand and remember a lot more easily.

5. Make your branches *curved* rather than straight lined. Why? Because having nothing but straight lines is boring to your brain.

6. Use *one key word per line*. Why? Because single key words give your mind map more power and flexibility.

7. Use *images* throughout. Why? Because each image, like the central image, is also worth a thousand words. So if you have only ten images in your mind map, it's already the equal of ten thousand words of notes!

Originated in the late 1960s by Tony Buzan, mind maps are now used by millions of people around the world—from the very young to the very old—whenever they wish to use their minds more effectively.

CHAPTER ONE

1. When economists use the term *public good*, they are describing a product or service with very specific characteristics: first, it costs no more to provide the good to many persons than it does to provide it to one, because one person's enjoyment of the good does not interfere with the ability of others to enjoy it; second, once the good has been provided to one person, there is no easy way to prevent others from consuming it as well. By this definition, national defense and radio broadcasts are examples of public good.

2. The summary of general participation theory is drawn from Berger and Neuhaus (1977). General participation theory has been one of the most significant intellectual influences on domestic policy and nonprofit sector practice over the past thirty years. Berger and Neuhaus introduced the now classic analysis that a healthy nation relies on the institutions of civil society—especially neighborhoods, families, churches, and voluntary associations—to mediate between individual citizens and the large bureaucratic "megastructures" of big government, big labor, and big business.

3. Skeletons function to support and give rigidity to organic forms and are generally inside the organism so that it can grow, develop, and change. The skeleton determines the basic form but not the details of tissue that make each organism unique. Similarly, the values and ideas we've pulled out from the theories about nonprofit organizations are like the skeleton

of many nonprofits' cultures, but in and of themselves aren't the end of the description of a particular organization's culture.

CHAPTER FOUR

1. For information about the ETM framework and leadership transition, visit the Annie E. Casey Foundation Web site (www.aecf.org) or Transition Guides (www.transitionguides.com). Leaders in developing the ETM framework were Tom Adams and Don Tebbe of TransitionGuides; Tim Wolfred of CompassPoint; Victor Chears of Chears & Associates; Joe Gonzalez of NeighborWorks America; Denice Hinden of Managance Consulting & Coaching; Paige Teegarden of Think Outside; and Karen Gaskins Jones of JLH Associates.

BIBLIOGRAPHY

Alinsky, S. (1971). *Rules for Radicals.* New York: Vintage Books.

Allport, G. W. (1948). "Foreword." In G. W. Lewin (Ed.), *Resolving Social Conflict.* London: HarperCollins.

Alvesson, M., and Berg, P. O. (1992). *Corporate Culture and Organizational Symbolism: An Overview.* Berlin: de Gruyter.

Argyris, C. (1996). "Actionable Knowledge: Intent Versus Actuality." *Journal of Applied Behavior Science, 32*(4), 441–445.

Argyris, C. (1997). "Learning and Teaching: A Theory of Action Perspective." *Journal of Management Education, 21*(1), 9–27.

Ashkanasy, N. M., Wilderom, C.P.M., and Peterson, M. F. (Eds.). (2000). *Handbook of Organizational Culture and Climate.* Thousand Oaks, CA: Sage.

Barrett, R. (2003). "Improve Your Cultural Capital." *Industrial Management,* Sept.-Oct. http://www.entrepreneur.com/tradejournals/article/110267350.html.

Beitler, M. (2003). *Strategic Organizational Change.* Greensboro, NC: Practitioner Press International.

Bennis, W. (1989). *On Becoming a Leader.* Reading, MA: Addison-Wesley.

Berger, P., and Neuhaus, R. (1977). *To Empower People: The Role of Mediating Structures in Public Policy.* Washington, DC: American Enterprise Institute.

Block, S. R. (1990). "A History of the Discipline." In D. L. Gies, S. Ott, and J. Shafritz (Eds.), *The Nonprofit Organization: Essential Readings.* Pacific Grove, CA: Brooks/Cole.

Block, S. R. (2004). *Why Nonprofits Fail: Overcoming Founder's Syndrome, Fundphobia, and Other Obstacles to Success.* San Francisco: Jossey-Bass.

Blumenthal, B. (2003). *Investing in Capacity Building: A Guide to High Impact Approaches.* New York: Foundation Center.

Bobbe, R. A., Dina, R. P., and Mickulas, P. M. (2004). "Leading While Learning in a Time of Tumultuous Change." *Journal for Nonprofit Management, 8*(1), 13–25.

Boyd, B. L. (2004). "Barriers to the Development of Volunteer Leadership Competencies: Why Johnnie Can't Lead Volunteers." *Journal of Volunteer Administration, 22*(4), 17–22.

Bridges, W. (2000). *The Character of Organizations: Using Personality Type in Organization Development.* Palo Alto, CA: Davies-Black.

Buzan, T., and Buzan, B. (1996). *The Mind Map Book: How to Use Radiant Thinking to Maximize Your Brain's Untapped Potential.* New York: Penguin Group.

Carleton, J. R., and Lineberry, C. (2004). *Achieving Post-Merger Success: A Stakeholder's Guide to Cultural Due Diligence, Assessment, and Integration.* San Francisco: Pfeiffer.

Carlson, M., and Donohoe, M. (2003). *The Executive Director's Survival Guide.* San Francisco: Jossey-Bass.

Checco, L. (2005). *Branding for Success!* Victoria, BC: Trafford.

Clemenson, B. (2006, March 2). "Stewardship in Nonprofit Organizations (Part I)." *Nonprofit Boards and Governance Review.* CharityChannel, http://charitychannel.com. (Available with CharityChannel membership).

Cnaan, R. A., Sinha, J. W., and McGrew, C. C. (2004). "Congregations as Social Service Providers: Services, Capacity, Culture, and Organizational Behavior." *Administration in Social Work, 28*(3), 47–68.

Collins, J. C., and Porras, J. I. (1994). *Built to Last: Successful Habits of Visionary Companies.* New York: Harper Business.

Connolly, P., and York, P. (2003). "Building the Capacity of Capacity Builders: A Study of Management Support and Field Building Organizations in the Nonprofit Sector." http://www.tccgrp.com/pubs/capacity.php. (Available by subscription to TCC Group).

Corlett, J. G., and Pearson, C. S. (2003). *Mapping the Organizational Psyche.* Gainesville, FL: Center for Applications of Psychological Type.

Curran, C. J. (2005). "Organizational Culture: The Path to Better Organizations." *Journal for Nonprofit Management, 9*(1), 28–40. http://www.carolynjcurran.com/pdf/ORGCULTURE.pdf.

Deal, T. E., and Kennedy, A. A. (1982). *Corporate Cultures: The Rites and Rituals of Corporate Life.* Reading, MA: Addison-Wesley.

Denison, D. R. (1990). *Corporate Culture and Organizational Effectiveness.* Hoboken, NJ: Wiley.

Denison, D. R., Hooijberg, R., and Quinn, R. E. (1995). "Paradox and Performance: Toward a Theory of Behavioral Complexity in Managerial Leadership." *Organizational Science, 6*(4), 524–540.

Douglas, J. (1987). "Political Theories of Nonprofit Organization." In W. W. Powell (Ed.), *The Nonprofit Sector: A Research Handbook.* New Haven, CT: Yale University Press.

Drucker, P. F. (1999). *The Drucker Foundation Self-Assessment Tool.* (Rev. ed.) San Francisco: Jossey-Bass.

Drucker, P. F. (2006). *Managing the Non-Profit Organization: Practices and Principles.* New York: HarperCollins.

Drucker, P. F. (2008). *The Five Most Important Questions You Will Ever Ask About Your Organization.* San Francisco: Jossey-Bass.

Fernandez, S., and Rainey, H. G. (2006). "Managing Successful Organizational Change in the Public Sector: An Agenda for Research and Practice." *Public Administration Review, 66*(2), 1–25.

French, W., and Bell, C. (1978). *Organizational Development: Behavioral Science Interventions for Organizational Improvement.* (2nd ed.) Upper Saddle River, NJ: Prentice Hall.

Geertz, C. (1973). *The Interpretation of Cultures.* New York: Basic Books.

Gallos, J. V. (Ed.). (2006). *Organization Development: A Jossey-Bass Reader.* San Francisco: Jossey-Bass.

Golden-Biddle, K., and Linduff, H. (1994). "Culture and Human Resources Management: Selecting Leadership in a Nonprofit Organization." *Nonprofit Management and Leadership, 4*(3), 301–315.

Hall, H. (2007, May 31). "Advancing Nonprofit Careers." *Chronicle of Philanthropy Special Report,* http://philanthropy.com/article/Advancing-Nonprofit-Careers/55412/. (Available by subscription to *Chronicle of Philanthropy*).

Hall, P. D. (1990). "Conflicting Managerial Cultures in Nonprofit Organizations." *Nonprofit Management and Leadership, 1*(2), 153–166.

Hammack, D. C. (Ed.). (1998). *Making the Nonprofit Sector in the United States.* Bloomington: Indiana University Press.

Haney, J. (2001). *Making Culture Pay: Solving the Puzzle of Organizational Effectiveness.* Lee's Summit, MO: Visionomics.

Hansmann, H. (1987). "Economic Theories of Nonprofit Organization." In W. W. Powell (Ed.), *The Nonprofit Sector: A Research Handbook.* New Haven, CT: Yale University Press.

Heifetz, R. A., and Linsky, M. (2002). *Leadership on the Line: Staying Alive Through the Dangers of Leading.* Boston: Harvard Business School Publishing.

Herzlinger, R. E. (1999). "Culture Is the Key." In F. Hesselbein, M. Goldsmith, and I. Somerville (Eds.), *Leading Beyond the Walls.* New York: Drucker Foundation.

Hesselbein, F. (2001, Fall). "A Splendid Torch." *Leader to Leader, 22,* 4–5. http://www.pfdf .org/knowledgecenter/journal.aspx?ArticleID5111.

James, R. (2004). "Exploring OD in Africa: A Response to David Lewis." *Nonprofit Management and Leadership, 14*(3), 313–324.

Jaskyte, K. (2004). "Transformational Leadership, Organizational Culture, and Innovation in Nonprofit Organizations." *Nonprofit Management and Leadership, 15*(2), 153–168.

Jaskyte, K., and Dressier, W. W. (2005). "Organizational Culture and Innovation in Nonprofit Human Service Organizations." *Administration in Social Work, 29*(2), 23–43.

Kotter, J., and Heskett, J. L. (1992). *Corporate Culture and Performance.* New York: Free Press.

Kotter, J., and Rathgeber, H. (2006). *Our Iceberg Is Melting.* New York: St. Martin's Press.

Knauft, E. B., Berger, R. A., and Gray, S. T. (1991). *Profiles of Excellence: Achieving Success in the Nonprofit Sector.* San Francisco: Jossey-Bass.

LaPiana, D. (2000). *The Nonprofit Mergers Workbook.* St. Paul, MN: A. H. Wilder Foundation.

LaPiana, D. (2008). *The Nonprofit Strategy Revolution: Real-Time Strategic Planning in a Rapid-Response World.* St. Paul, MN: Fieldstone Alliance.

LaPiana, D., et. al. (2004). *The Nonprofit Mergers Workbook Part II: Unifying the Organization After a Merger.* St. Paul, MN: Fieldstone Alliance.

Lewin, K. (1948). *Resolving Social Conflicts.* New York: HarperCollins.

Lewis, D. J. (2003, November). "Rethinking Sustainable Development: NGOs, Organizational Culture, and Institutional Sustainability." *Annals of the American Academy of Political and Social Science, 590*(1), 73–92.

Light, P. C. (2002). *Pathways to Nonprofit Excellence.* Washington, DC: Brookings Institution.

Linden, R. M. (2002). "Toward a Collaborative Culture." *Working Across Boundaries.* San Francisco: Jossey-Bass.

Mark, M., and Pearson, C. S. (2001). *The Hero and the Outlaw: Building Extraordinary Brands Through the Power of Archetypes.* New York: McGraw-Hill.

Mattessich, P. W. (2003). *The Manager's Guide to Program Evaluation: Planning, Contracting, and Managing for Useful Results.* St. Paul, MN: A. H. Wilder Foundation.

McLaughlin, T. A. (1998). *Nonprofit Mergers and Alliances: A Strategic Planning Guide.* Hoboken, NJ: Wiley.

Morey, N., and Luthans, F. (1985). "Refining the Displacement of Culture and the Use of Scenes and Themes in Organizational Studies." *Academy of Management Review, 10*(2), 219–229.

Morgan, G. (1986). *Images of Organizations.* Thousand Oaks, CA: Sage.

Nelson, G. M., Salmon, M.A.P., and Howell, C. (2002). *Assessing the Human Services Culture: Open Systems Management.* Vol. 1. Victoria, BC: Trafford.

Netting, F. E., Nelson, H. W., Jr., and Borders, K. (2004). "Volunteer and Paid Staff Relationships: Implications for Social Work Administration." *Administration in Social Work, 28*(3), 111–136.

Oleck, H. (1988). *Nonprofit Corporations, Organizations, and Associations.* Upper Saddle River, NJ: Prentice Hall.

Ott, J. S. (1989). *The Organizational Cultural Perspective.* Belmont, CA: Dorsey Press.

Pearson, C. S. (1998). *The Hero Within: Six Archetypes We Live By.* San Francisco: HarperCollins.

Pearson, C. S. (2003). *Archetypes in Organizational Settings: A Client's Guide to the OTCI Professional Report.* Gainesville, FL: Center for Applications of Psychological Type.

Pearson, C. S. (2003). *Understanding Archetypes in Your Organization: An Introduction to the OTCI Basic Report.* Gainesville, FL: Center for Applications of Psychological Type.

Pearson C. S., and Marr, H. K. (2002). *Introduction to Archetypes: A Companion for Understanding and Using the Pearson-Marr Archetype Indicator Instrument.* Gainesville, FL: Center for Applications of Psychological Type.

Peters, T. J., and Waterman, R. H. (1982). *In Search of Excellence: Lessons from America's Best-Run Companies.* New York: HarperCollins.

Schein, E. H. (1992). "Defining Organizational Culture." In J. Shafritz and S. Ott (Eds.), *Classics of Organization Theory.* Pacific Grove, CA: Brooks/Cole. (Originally published in E. H. Schein, *Organizational Culture and Leadership* [San Francisco: Jossey-Bass, 1985], pp. 1–22).

Schein, E. H. (1999). *The Corporate Culture Survival Guide: Sense and Nonsense About Cultural Change.* San Francisco: Jossey-Bass.

Schein, E. H. (2004). *Organizational Culture and Leadership.* (3rd ed.) San Francisco: Jossey-Bass.

Shafritz, J., and Ott, S. (1992). *Classics of Organization Theory.* Pacific Grove, CA: Brooks/Cole.

Sherriton, J., and Stern, J. (1997). *Corporate Culture/Team Culture: Removing Hidden Barriers to Team Success.* New York: American Management Association.

Simon, J. S., and Donovan, T. (2001). *The Five Life Stages of Nonprofit Organizations: Where You Are, Where You're Going, and What to Expect When You Get There.* St. Paul, MN: A. H. Wilder Foundation.

Starcevich, M. M. (2009). Review of *Diagnosing and Changing Organizational Culture: Based on the Competing Values Framework,* by Kim S. Cameron and Robert E. Quinn. http://www.coachingandmentoring.com/BookReviews/diagnosingculture.htm.

Stevens, S. K. (2002). *Nonprofit Lifecycles: Stage-Based Wisdom for Nonprofit Capacity.* Long Lake, MN: Stagewise Enterprises.

Thomas, H., Leslie, D., and Holzhalb, C. (1993). "Culture and Change in Nonprofit Boards." *Nonprofit Management and Leadership, 4*(2), 141–155.

Trice, H., and Beyer, J. (1993). *The Cultures of Work Organizations.* Upper Saddle River, NJ: Prentice Hall.

Vroom, V. H., and Maier, N.R.F. (1961). "Industrial Social Psychology." *Annual Review of Psychology, 12,* 413–446.

Weiss, R. (2008, September). "Q&A with Edgar Schein: Defining a Company Culture." *ASTD Consulting News, 2*(3).

ABOUT THE AUTHORS

Paige Hull Teegarden, MPP, has more than fifteen years of experience building the effectiveness of a wide range of organizations. As president of Think Outside (www.ThinkOutside.net), she leads innovative strategy, team, and leadership development with nonprofits, government agencies, small businesses, and collaborations. With a focus on creative strategy development, Think Outside offers strategic planning, organization review and support in the context of organizational culture, and corporate team building and staff development.

Paige is a systems thinker with an uncanny ability to ask the questions that help organizations think strategically. She has facilitated strategic planning processes for multimillion-dollar organizations; helped start-up volunteer organizations and businesses create their structure and processes; and designed and conducted significant research studies, including the first-ever competency study of leaders facilitating community-building initiatives and the largest survey on nonprofit sector executive transitions. She has also designed and supported the implementation of evaluation systems that allow organizations to gather information about their performance and their impact. She is a gifted facilitator with an interest in using outdoor experiences and our connection to the natural world to create new perspective and breakthrough strategies. Paige has an MA in public policy from Johns Hopkins University and a BA in political science from Davidson College, North Carolina.

Denice Rothman Hinden, PhD, ACC, has more than twenty-five years of experience in nonprofit management, organization development, research, group facilitation, and professional coaching. As president of Managance Consulting & Coaching (www.managance.com), she facilitates bold strategic thinking and planning; business planning; and leader, team, board, and group development, with attention to group process and individual responsibility. The firm's clients include nonprofits, coalitions, philanthropies, government agencies, libraries, and small businesses.

Denice thinks about organizations holistically, paying attention to the relationship between the identity of an organization—including its mission, vision, core operating values, theory of action, customers and organizational culture, influences in its environment—and operating capacity. Denice is an accomplished facilitator with a track record of asking powerful questions and creating distinct strategies that move organizations and individuals to new levels of success. She was part of the pioneering team that introduced nonprofits to executive transition management.

Denice began her nonprofit sector career as a volunteer crisis counselor on a suicide prevention hotline and later directed the construction and operations of two emergency shelters for runaway and homeless youth in Miami. She is a graduate of CoachU and an Associate Certified Coach through the International Coach Federation. Denice holds a PhD in public administration from Florida International University, an MS in human services from Nova Southeastern University, and a BA in urban studies and Latin American studies from the University of Pittsburgh.

Paul Sturm, MPA, MS, has worked on the cutting edge of nonprofit leadership development and capacity building for more than twenty-five years. He founded and led two organizations nationally recognized for their innovations and outcomes. He has served as consultant to nonprofit and capacity-building organizations throughout the United States. His groundbreaking article, "The Seven Rules of Successful Collaboration," was published in *Nonprofit World* in 2000. Paul has presented workshops on collaboration and peer learning at several national and statewide conferences of nonprofit leaders and capacity builders. He teaches in the Community Studies and Civic Engagement Program at the University of Baltimore and the Nonprofit Management Program at the College of Notre Dame of Maryland. Paul also coordinates and facilitates the Baltimore Nonprofit Leaders Circles and presents workshops for the Maryland Association of Nonprofit Organizations and Delaware Association of Nonprofit Agencies. Paul earned an MPA from the Harvard Kennedy School, an MS in urban affairs from the University of Wisconsin, and a BA in urban studies and communications from Syracuse University.

ACKNOWLEDGMENTS

This book would not have been possible without the generosity, encouragement, and feedback of a lot of people who believed in our vision of the first book dedicated to organizational culture in the nonprofit sector. Our early encouragers include Heather Iliff, then with the Alliance for Nonprofit Management; Bill Ryan at Harvard's Hauser Center for Nonprofit Organizations; Kathleen Enright of Grantmakers for Effective Organizations; Paul Light at New York University; Dave Renz at the University of Missouri-Kansas City's Midwest Center for Nonprofit Leadership; Brian Fraser of JazzThink; and Vince Hyman and Carol Lukas at Fieldstone Alliance. The participants in our roundtable discussions at the Alliance for Nonprofit Management conferences and other colleagues in the nonprofit capacity-building community provided an invaluable sounding board and encouragement as well.

We also thank the following people for sharing their stories and perspectives as we worked to discover the hidden truths of organizational culture in the nonprofit sector: Jamie Alvarado of Somos Mayfair; Heather Berthoud, Berthoud Greene Associates; Stephen Block of Denver Options and the University of Colorado; Peter Brinckerhoff, Corporate Alternatives; Lisa Buttner; Janet Froetscher, formerly with United Way of Metropolitan Chicago; Amy Ginsburg of Manna Food Center; Manny Hidalgo of Latin American Economic Development Corporation; Robert Hoffman; Ruth McCambridge of the *Nonprofit Quarterly*; Steven McCullough of Bethel New Life; Richard Moyers of the Eugene and Agnes E. Meyer Foundation; Sarah Basehart Sorenson of the Arc of Maryland; and Claudia Thorne of Community Life Services.

Special thanks to the devoted and wise staff at Fieldstone Alliance and Jossey-Bass—Rebecca Post, Allison Brunner, Byron Schneider, and Dani Scoville—for their guidance and support for three first-time book authors. An additional note of gratitude is in order for Vince Hyman, our first editor. With patience and insightful questions, you all helped us make the book more accessible. Our readers will be richer as a result of your pushing our thinking and writing to another level. Thank you!

INDEX

Culture creation, 11; leaders' influence on, 12, 23, 37–39, 117–118, 146–147, 148; during organization formation, 9, 23, 52–53, 69, 133–134. *See also* Creation stories

Culture description: approaches to, 99, 101–103, 104–107; implications of, understanding the, 64–65, 112, 113–114; using, for management strategies, 123–134, 138; writing the, 103, 108, 109–110

Culture discovery, 69–122; description and analysis step in, 99–111; facilitation of, 74; general guidelines for, 74–75; intuition in, 75, 101; objective for engaging in, 77–78, 80–81, 83, 112; ongoing use of, 123–134, 138; outside capacity builders' assistance in, 135–137; preliminary considerations for, 74–75; preparation phase of, 76–78, 79–81; Revealing Organizational Culture (ROC) process for, 75–122; story collection and interpretation for, 79, 81–111; stress and, 33–35; time required for, 69, 122; tools for, 70, 149–151; using stories for, 33, 63–67, 70, 71–75; willingness to engage in, 74, 136–137. *See also* Revealing Organizational Culture (ROC)

Customers. *See* Clients or customers

D

Daring to Lead 2006 (Moyers et al.), 144

Data collection: about organization and context, 76–78; about organizational identity, 76–77; written summary of, 79–81

De Pree, M., 74

Decentralized leadership, 20, 46–49, 61–63

Decision making: analysis of, 103, 106, 110; decentralizing, 47–48, 51, 61–63; participative, 15, 19, 29, 121; quick, crisis-oriented, 90, 106, 108, 109, 110, 121

Democracy, 14, 15

Denison, D. R., 149, 150

Denison Organizational Culture Survey (DOCS), 149, 150

Denisonculture.com, 150

Denver Options, 134, 142

"DevCorps" case example, 54–59, 65–67

Developmental disability organization, 127, 130–131

Diagnosing Organizational Culture (Harrison and Stokes), 151

Dialectic change theory, 99

Dissonance, 99, 100, 118

Distributed or decentralized leadership, 20, 46–49, 61–63

Diversity: among Latino groups, 62; civic diversity theory and, 14, 15, 19; as common nonprofit value, 28; community-based service organizations and, 25–26; solidarity and, 15, 19, 28

Domestic violence shelter, success stories from, 146

Douglas, J., 14, 15

Dress, artifact of, 85, 96

Drucker, P., 74, 127, 128, 140

Duty of obedience, 16, 17

E

Economic development districts, innovation theory and, 16

Economic theories of nonprofit existence, 13–14, 18. *See also* Contract failure theory; Provision of public good theory

Effectiveness, organizational culture and, 2–3

Efficiency: changing culture for, 56–59; flexibility and, 29

Emergency succession planning, 131

Entrepreneurial values, 46, 47, 48

Environment, assumptions about, 103, 107

Environmental change. *See* External change

Equine-assisted activities, 120–121

Equity: community-based service organizations and, 24; as nonprofit value, 28; provision of public good theory and, 14, 18, 97

Espoused values: analysis of, 11; defined, 9; dissonance between behavior and, 99, 100, 118–119; examples of, 26, 95; gathering and mapping, 84–85, 95

Evaluation, program, 130–131

Excellence, culture change for, in case example, 51–55

Executive director transition: case examples of, 45–54, 61–63; Executive Transition Management (ETM) framework for, 131–132, 156*n*. 1; as nonprofit stressor, 34, 45, 66; opportunities in, 45. *See also* Founders; Leaders; Leadership change

Executive Transition Management (ETM) framework, 131–132, 156*n*. 1

Experiential training, 120–121

External change: case examples of, 54–63; as nonprofit stressor, 34, 54, 66–67

External survival, assumptions about, 10–11

F

Facebook, 21

Facilitation, of culture discovery process: benefits of, 74; in culture description/analysis step, 99, 111; and mind mapping, 85, 87, 89, 91, 153–154; in story collection/mind mapping step, 82, 85, 89, 91, 98–99

Fairness: as common nonprofit value, 28; community-based service organizations and, 24; provision of public good theory and, 14, 18, 97

Faith-Based Management (Brinckerhoff), 142

Faith-based organizations, 45–49, 65. *See also* "Human Rights Institute (HRI)" case example

Feedback loops, 119–120

Fernandez, S., 99

Fieldstone Alliance, 143

Fighting style, 37–39, 147–148

Financial Empowerment (Brinckerhoff), 142

Financial systems: changing, in executive director transition, 47, 48; focus on, in response to funding change, 56–59

501(c)(3) organizations, 16–17, 19

Flexibility, nonprofit: as common nonprofit value, 28; of community-based service organizations, 25; efficiency and, 29; innovation theory and, 15–16, 19, 66

Food distribution organization. *See* Manna Food Center

Formal or "overt" issues, in organizational iceberg, 27, 34

Foundations, innovation theory and, 16

Founders: aftermath of death of, 72–73; change-resistant, in case example, 35–39; cultural influence of, 12, 23, 37–39, 117–118, 146–147, 148; executive director transition from, 45–49, 66. *See also* Executive director transition; Leaders

Free riders, 14, 18

Fund for the Homeless, 144

Funding: identifying sources of, 77; impact of changes in, 54–59, 66–67; organizational image and, 127, 129–130

Fundraising, balancing, with mission, 21

G

Gallos, J. V., 117

General participation theory, 15, 90, 155*n*. 2

Generations (Brinckerhoff), 142

Ginsburg, A., 50–55, 118

God's providence, belief in, 48, 65, 107

Government bureaucracy, 15

Government by the People (Light), 143

Government contracting, consortium, 56–57

Government relationships: community-based service organizations in, 25; conflict avoidance approach to, 104, 109; innovation theory organizations in, 16, 19

Greenpeace, 10, 14

Group process, 119, 120–121

H

Hall, H., 22

Hansmann, H., 13

Hard work, belief in, 24–25, 48

Harrison, R., 151

Health care management field, 22

Heaven, reward in, 104

Heifetz, R. A., 74, 118, 136

Hero and the Outlaw, The (Mark and Pearson), 130

Hero mentality, 24–25

Hero or heroine stories. *See* "Successful staff person" stories

Heskett, J. L., 8–9

Hesselbein, F., 140

Hewlett Foundation, William and Flora, 40, 41, 43, 44

Hidalgo, M., 60–63

Hinden, D., 128

Hoffman, R., 142–143, 146

Hoffman, Robert, & Associates, 142

Homeless youth organization, 72–73

Homeownership, promotion of, 60–63

Human dignity, inconsistent respect for, 100, 108, 109, 110

Human nature, underlying assumptions about, 10, 103, 107

"Human Rights Institute (HRI)" case example, 70; action plan approach of, 116–117; culture summary of, 109–110; inconsistencies explanation in, 108; inconsistencies identification in, 100; mind map of, 91, 92–93; new objective of, 125, 126; nonprofit theories and values applied to, 97–98; objective and implications step in, 113–114, 125, 126; preliminary objective of, 83; preparation phase of, written summary, 79–81; story narratives of, 94–96; theme analysis in, 104–107; theme identification in, 98

Human service nonprofit organizations, 1

Human Synergistics, Inc., 151

Humansynergistics.com, 151

I

Iceberg image, 26–28, 34, 90–91, 137

Image building (organizational), 127, 129–130

Images: archetypal, 130; in mind map, 90–91

Imagination Stage, 144

Immigrant empowerment, 42–44, 59–63

Immigrant worldview, 42–44, 65

Implementation planning, 115, 117–121. *See also* Action plan; Culture change

Inconsistencies: explaining, 103, 108; identification of, 99, 100; reflection on, 118–119

Informal or "covert" issues, in organizational iceberg, 27, 34

Information asymmetry, 14

Information use and exchange, 58, 87, 96, 102, 105

Innovation: as common nonprofit value, 28, 29; in development nonprofit case example, 56–59, 66–67; efficiency and, 28

Innovation theory: community-based service organizations and, 25; elements of, 15–16, 65–66; values associated with, 19

Integration. *See* Internal integration; Racial integration

Interaction: analysis of, 102, 104; underlying assumptions about, 10

Interfaith Works. *See* Community Ministries

Internal integration, assumptions and, 10–11

Internal reorganization, 132

Internal Revenue Service (IRS) categories, 16

International scholarship organization, 54

Internet: culture diagnostic instrument on, 150–151; as nonprofit organizing and networking tool, 21–22

Interviews, top management, in preparation phase, 77–78, 80–81

Intuition: to discover themes, 64; to draft underlying assumptions, 101; role of, in culture discovery, 75

Issues, organizational, identification of, 77, 80

J

"Just do it" value, 50, 51, 52–53

Process issues, in organizational iceberg, 27, 34
Professional background, as artifact, 85, 96
Professionalism, nonprofit, 22–23
Program evaluation, 130–131
Promotores, 42
Provision of public good theory: community-based service organizations and, 24; elements of, 13–14; values associated with, 18, 97
Public good, defined, 155*n*. 1. *See also* Provision of public good theory
Public radio, 14
Punishment, analysis of, 87, 102, 105

Q
Qualitative approach, to culture diagnosis, 149–150
Quality focus: nondistribution constraint and, 16–17, 19; as nonprofit commonality, 29
Quantity focus: nondistribution constraint and, 16–17, 19; as nonprofit commonality, 29

R
Racial integration, 25–26, 49
Racial justice, beliefs and values about, 25–26, 49
Rainey, H. G., 99
RAND Corporation, 10
Rathgeber, H., 26
Realignment, 132
Reflection: leadership's, 118–119; points of, in action plan, 119–120
Reilly, C. A., 151
Religious hierarchy, obedience to, 104, 108
Renz, D., 145, 146
Rescue training activity, 121
Research, nonprofit culture: agenda for future, 139; dearth of, 8
Restructuring, 132–134
Revealing Organizational Culture (ROC), 1, 3–5, 33; action planning step in, 112, 114–115, 116–117, 119; bases and development of, 70, 123, 141, 149; for capacity building, 124–125, 126, 135–138; for closing an organization, 133–134; culture diagnostic tools and, 70, 149–151; defining organization culture in, 83; facilitator for, 74; implementation planning step in, 115, 117–121; implications step of, 112, 113–114, 125, 126; for logic model development, 130–131; for marketing and image building, 127, 129–130; objective identification and description in, 77–78, 80–81, 83; objective review in, 112; ongoing uses of, 123–134, 138; overview of phases in, 75–76; participation in, 70, 79, 81, 119; phase 1 (preparation) of, 75, 76–78, 79–81; phase 2 (gather stories and interpret) of, 75, 78, 81–111, 124; phase 3 (assess implications/create action plan) of, 75–76, 112–115, 124–125; phase 4 (define action and implementation),

76, 117–121, 155; preliminary considerations for, 74–75; process of, 75–122; for program evaluation, 130–131; for restructuring, 132–134; for start-up culture creation, 133–134; for strategic planning, 125, 126, 128–129; for succession planning, 131–132; using, in organization development, 123–134
Revealorganizationalculture.com, 6, 138
Rewards, analysis of, 87, 102, 104. *See also* Salaries
Riots, organizations born out of, 46, 49, 60, 62
Risk and benefit analysis, 64–65, 99, 108–111
ROC. *See* Revealing Organizational Culture
Rules, attitudes toward, 51–52, 53
Rules for Radicals (Alinsky), 24
Rural development organization, 54–55
Russia, nonprofit management education in, 141, 142

S
Salaries, expectation for low, 24–25, 96, 97, 110–111
San Jose, California, 40
Schein, E., 9, 10, 30, 70, 99, 117, 120, 149–150
Service delivery improvement, 51–55, 131
Service learning, 20
"Shifting the Organization's Culture: A Self-Assessment Guide," 151
Shutdown, organization, 123, 133–134
Silicon valley Community Foundation, 40
Skeletons, 17–18, 155*n*. 3
Social capital, 43–44
Social enterprise, 20
Social Entrepreneurship (Brinckerhoff), 142
Social networking, 21–22
Social venture capital, 20
Socratic seminars, 10
Solidarity, diversity and, 15, 19, 28
Somos Mayfair, 40–44, 64, 65, 118
Space, underlying assumptions about, 10
Staff, nonprofit: altruistic motivation of, 29, 96, 109–110; clients as, 50–55, 97, 110, 111; from community, 49, 50; executive director transition and, 45, 47, 50–55; low salary expectations for, 24–25, 96, 97, 110–111; new, 120; professional backgrounds of, 85, 96; resistance of, overcoming, 47, 51–55, 64, 115–116; retaining and rewarding, 61; stories of successful, 55, 73–75; turnover in, 77, 81
Stevens, S. K., 35
Stokes, H., 151
Stories: of community-based development organization, 41–42; creating new, 125; example, 94–96; facilitation of, 82, 85, 89, 91, 98–99; gathering and interpreting, 75, 78, 81–82, 81–111; group discussion on, 78, 81–111; images from, 90–91; listening to, 82, 89, 136, 145–146, 148; meeting agenda for, 81–82; mind mapping, 84–97; of organizational success, 42, 55, 120, 146; questions for

Printed and bound by CPI Group (UK) Ltd, Croydon, CR0 4YY

16/04/2025

14658529-0001